Survey of Student Retention Policies in Higher Education

ISBN: 1-57440-097-5

1

Survey Participants

Appalachian State
Austin Peay State University
Bacone College
Bates College
Bow Valley College
California Lutheran University
California State University Long Beach
Carolinas College of Health Sciences
Chicago State University
Global College
Iowa State University - Dean of Students Office
Kirtland Community College
Lynn University
McKendree University
Monmouth University
Moraine Park Technical College
Morgan State University
Mount Olive College
Neumann College
New York University
Ohio Dominican University
Randolph College
Raritan Valley Community College
Richland Community College
Robert Morris University
San Jose State University
Schreiner University
Southwestern University
SUNY College at Old Westbury
UCCS
University of South Carolina
University of Arizona
University of Arkansas at Pine Bluff
University of Central Florida
University of Guelph
University of Illinois at Chicago Honors College
Virginia Commonwealth University
WV Northern Community College
Youngstown State University

Table of Contents

List of Tables

Demographics of the Sample

Public/Private Status

	Public College	Private College
Entire Sample	65.00%	35.00%

FTE Enrollment

	Under 2,000 FTE Enrollment	2,000 To 10,000 FTE Enrollment	10,000+ FTE Enrollment
Entire Sample	35.00%	37.50%	27.50%

Type Of College

	Community College	4-Year Or MA Degree Granting Institution	PhD Granting Institution Or Research University
Entire Sample	17.50%	62.50%	20.00%

Mean, Median, Minimum And Maximum Full Time Equivalent Enrollment

	Mean	Median	Minimum	Maximum
Entire Sample	8211.64	3100.00	0.00	48000.00

Mean, Median, Minimum And Maximum Full Time Equivalent Enrollment, Broken Out By Type Of College

Type Of College	Mean	Median	Minimum	Maximum
Community College	2428.57	1800.00	300.00	6500.00
4-Year Or MA Degree Granting Institution	7260.96	3500.00	100.00	29800.00
PhD Granting Institution Or Research University	21375.00	25500.00	1400.00	48000.00

Summary of Main Findings

Spending on Retention Consulting Services

Colleges in the sample spent a mean of $25,527 on consulting services for student retention in the past year. Most colleges spent nothing; however, one college spent as much as one-half million dollars. As might be expected, public colleges spent significantly more than private colleges; public colleges in the sample spent a mean of $41,357 per year, while private colleges spent a shade more than $6,900 per year. PhD-level and research universities spent the most, a mean of $49,000 per year, while community colleges spent the least, a shade over $3,916 per year. The colleges in the sample expected to spend less in the coming year on consulting services to aid in retention, a mean of $14,027 with a maximum of $275,000. Private colleges expected to spend virtually nothing, a mean of only $1,591, while public colleges plan to spend more than $24,000 per year on consulting services to aid in student retention. For the coming year, spending plans were closely related to college size; colleges with enrollment of under 2,000 FTE plan to spend a shade more than $225, virtually nothing. Colleges with enrollment greater than 10,000 FTE plan to spend nearly $41,000 per year. Community colleges plan to spend less than $3,600, while PhD-granting or research universities plan to spend $59,000, on average. Four-year and MA-granting institutions plan to spend $9,425 per year.

Spending on Publications, Conferences and Other Retention-Related Information

In the past year the colleges in the sample spent $9,696 on average on conferences, Webcasts, research reports and other specialized publications and information resources about student retention. One college spent as much as $100,000. Once again spending by public colleges was far greater than spending by private colleges by a factor of nearly three to one. Public colleges spent on average $15,028 while private colleges spent a little more than $5,200. As might be expected, spending is closely related to school size. Colleges with less than 2,000 FTE student enrollment spent a mean of $5,545 on conferences, publications, Webcasts and so on about student retention, while those with enrollment of greater than 10,000 spent a mean of $46,437. PhD-granting and research institutions spent nearly 4 times as much per year as four-year and MA-granting institutions, $31,200 compared to $8,207.

Percentage of Colleges with a Dean or other High-Level Administrator for Retention

65% of the colleges sampled had a high-level administrator or Dean whose primary responsibility is to maintain and increase student retention. Interestingly, though public colleges vastly outspent private colleges on consulting services in retention, more private colleges than public colleges had a Dean or other high-level administrator whose primary responsibility is to maintain and increase student retention. 61.54% of public colleges had such a position, while 71.43% of private colleges did. Community colleges and PhD-granting and research universities were much more likely to have such an administrator than were four-year or MA-granting institutions; more than 87% of PhD-granting or research universities had such an administrator, as did 71.43% of community colleges; however, only 56% of four-year and MA-granting institutions had a chief administrator in charge of retention.

Retention Rates for Full-Time Students

The mean retention rate for the fall semester 2006 to the fall semester 2007 for the colleges in the sample was 73.8%; the median was virtually exactly the same at 74%. The range was quite extraordinary; it went from 45% to 98%. Interestingly, and unexpectedly from our point of view, retention rates were higher among the larger schools in the sample. For colleges with more than 10,000 students FTE, retention rates were close to 83%, while the colleges with under 2000 FTE enrollment had retention rates that were a shade less than 69%. PhD-granting and research universities had higher retention rates than other types of institutions; their rates were close to 84%, while rates for other colleges averaged a shade more than 71%.

Retention Rates for Part-Time Students

Retention rates for part-time students were lower than retention rates for full-time students, but just slightly. Retention rates for part-time students averaged 67.7%, with a median of 74%; the range was great: from 35% to 94%. Private colleges did far better than public colleges when it came to retaining part-time students. The private colleges had retention rates for part-time students of 92% while the public colleges had rates a shade less than 63%. One interesting finding is that the minimum retention rate for the private colleges in the sample for part-time students was 90% while the maximum rate for the public colleges in the sample was 85%. Retention rates for part-time students did not appear to be strongly related to college size. However, these rates were strongly linked to the type of college. Community colleges had very low retention rates for part-time students; indeed, the community colleges in our sample retained only 45% of the part-time students year-over-year, while the PhD-granting or research universities retained 84%.

Start to Finish Student Graduation Rates

The overall graduation rate for the colleges in the sample was 51%; that is, 51% of students who started the college as freshmen actually graduated from the college. The rate was dramatically broad, ranging from zero to 92%.

Once again, private colleges did somewhat better than the public colleges though not nearly as well as one might expect. 57% of students who started at a private college ultimately graduated from that same college. However, for the public colleges in the sample, only 49.53% of those who start the college finished with that same college. The larger colleges did best; 62.44% of the students who start at these colleges as freshmen graduate from the same college.

Criteria By which Colleges Track Retention Rates

65% of the colleges in the sample track retention rates by declared academic major. More than 73% of public colleges compile this data, while only half of the private colleges in the sample did so. Interestingly, community colleges were the most likely to track this data. Nearly 86% of the community colleges in the sample track retention rates by declared academic major. A mean of only approximately 61.25% of the other colleges in the sample track retention rates by academic major.

40 to 45% of the colleges in the sample track retention rates by grade point average or SAT level. There was no difference to the extent to which public colleges and private colleges track this information. However, only 14.3% of community colleges track graduation retention rates by grade point average or SAT score, while more than 62% of research universities do it.

65% of the colleges in the sample track retention rates by gender. Private colleges, and the larger colleges, those with more than 10,000 students FTE, were the most likely to track retention rates by gender, as were the research universities.

75% of the colleges in the sample track retention rates by race. Nearly 86% of the private colleges in the sample track retention rates by race, as did close to 91% of colleges with more than 10,000 students and 100% of the PhD-granting or research universities in the sample.

47.5% of the colleges in the sample track retention rates of transferees into the college. Interestingly, public colleges were more likely to do this than private colleges. Close to 54% of the public colleges in the sample track retention rates for transferees into the college, while 35.7% of the private colleges did so.

The Impact of Financial Aid on Student Retention

We asked the colleges in the sample to rank how certain critical factors affected their retention rates; for each factor the survey participants were given four potential answers: one: does not have much of an impact; two: has some impact; three: has a significant impact; and four: has a dramatic impact. The first question was what is the impact of student financial assistance on student retention? 5% said it does not have much of an impact 20% said it has some impact, 2.5% say it had a significant impact, and 32.5% say it has a dramatic impact. Interestingly, it is the PhD-granting or research institutions that feel that financial aid has the greatest impact. All of them felt that financial aid had a significant or dramatic impact on their retention rates.

The Impact of Severity of Grading on Student Retention

The second question we asked was: What is the impact of the level of severity in grading on student retention? 17.5% of the colleges sampled said it does not have much of an impact, while 55% said it had some impact. 20% noted that it had a significant impact and 7.5% said it had a dramatic impact. Public colleges were more likely than private colleges to say that the severity of grading had an impact on student retention. Close to 35% of public colleges said that severity of grading had a significant or dramatic impact on retention, while only a little more than 14% of private colleges said so.

The Impact of Access to Tutoring on Student Retention

17.5% of organizations sampled said that access to tutoring services does not have much of an impact on student retention; 32.5% said that it has some impact, while 37.5% said it had significant impact and 12.5% said it had a dramatic impact. More than 95% of public colleges said that tutoring services had an impact on student retention rates; more than 60% said it had either a significant or dramatic impact, more than double the rate for the private colleges. Interestingly, it was the PhD-granting and research universities that said tutoring had made the greatest difference; three-quarters of them said that tutoring has had a significant or dramatic impact on their retention rates.

The Impact of Academic/Psychological Counseling on Student Retention

Ninety percent of the colleges in the sample said that access to academic and/or psychological counseling services had an impact on their student retention rates; 40% said it had some impact, while 35% said it had a significant impact and 15% said it had a dramatic impact. Once again, the impact is greater for the public colleges than for the private colleges. Also, for the larger schools, more than 80% said that access to academic and/or psychological consulting counseling services had a significant or dramatic impact on retention rates.

The Impact of General Economic Conditions on Student Retention

Ten percent of the colleges in the sample said that general economic conditions do not have much of an impact on their retention rates; for 42.5%, it had some impact; 27.5% noted that it had a significant impact and 20% said it had a dramatic impact. As might be expected, public colleges said that economic conditions were much more likely to have an impact. 31% of public colleges said that economic conditions have a significant impact on student retention and 23.1% said it had a dramatic impact. Only 21.4% of private colleges said that it had a significant impact, and 14.3% said it had a dramatic impact. The community colleges were most affected by economic conditions. More than 85% of community colleges said that economic conditions had a significant or dramatic impact on student retention.

The Impact of Participation in Extra-Curricular Activities on Student Retention

10% of the colleges in the sample said that involvement in extra-curricular activities does not have much of an impact on student retention, while 42.5% said it had some impact and 30% said it had a significant impact. 17.5% noted that it had a dramatic impact on student retention. It was the private colleges that felt that involvement in extracurricular activities had the most impact on retention rates; close to 43% felt that involvement in extracurricular activities had a significant impact on retention rates while 21.4% felt it had a dramatic impact.

For the public colleges only 23.1% said it had a significant impact and 15.4% felt it had a dramatic impact. Unexpectedly, the larger colleges are less likely to feel that involvement in extracurricular activities had a dramatic impact on their retention rates; only 9.1% of them felt this way while more than 28% of colleges with fewer than 2,000 students felt this way. Four-year or MA-granting institutions were also the most likely to feel that involvement in extracurricular activities had a significant or dramatic impact on retention.

The Impact of the Quality of Residence Halls and Food Service on Student Retention

42.5% of colleges in the sample believed that the quality of residence halls and food service did not have much of an impact on student retention, while 37.5% felt it had some impact and 12.5% noted that it had a significant impact; only 7.5% said that it had a dramatic impact. Private colleges were much more likely than public colleges to feel that the quality of residence halls and food service had a significant or dramatic impact on retention. All of the community colleges in the sample believed that the quality of residence halls and food service had little impact on retention.

The Impact of Student Exit Interviews of Various Kinds on Student Retention

The colleges in the sample interviewed a mean of 26.1% of the students who decided to transfer out of the college prior to graduation. The range in this case is extraordinary, going from zero to 100% with a median of just 5%. Private colleges were far more likely than public colleges to interview students who had transferred out or dropped out of the college prior to graduation. Public colleges in the sample interviewed a mean of 16.6% of the students who left or dropped out prior to graduation; however, the private colleges interviewed a mean of nearly 42% of students who left or dropped out prior to graduation and a median of 37.5%.

The smaller the college, the more likely was the college to interview those who decided to leave or drop out. The colleges with fewer than 2,000 students interviewed a mean of 38.1% of those who left or dropped out, and a median of 25%; for colleges with more than 10,000 students, they interviewed a mean of 11.3% and median of just 1% of the students who dropped out or left.

The colleges in the sample interviewed a mean of 34% of students who graduated the college to find out about their experience at the college. The range was great, from zero to 100% with a median of 15%. There was less of a difference in this respect between the public colleges and the private colleges. The public colleges interviewed a mean of 33% of the recent graduates while the private colleges interviewed a mean of 35.6%. However, the median was somewhat higher for the private colleges, at 27.5%, but only 12% for the public colleges, suggesting that some public colleges interviewed a great many of their graduates but many of the public colleges did not interview any at all. The community colleges tend to interview a higher percentage of their graduates, a mean of 44.3%, while the average for other institutions was a bit more than 33%.

We asked the colleges in the sample to rate the importance for retention enhancement of exit interviews for departing students who did not graduate the college. We asked them how important this was in developing and implementing a retention strategy for the college. About 18.2% of the colleges in the sample said that this exercise was absolutely vital; another 18.2% considered it useful, while 30.3% considered it somewhat useful. About 24.2% said it was not really too useful and 9.1% noted that it was virtually useless. Private colleges were more likely to find this exercise useful; 25% said it was absolutely vital, while another 25% said it was useful and 41.7% said it was somewhat useful. For the public colleges, on the other hand, only 14.3% considered the interviews absolutely invaluable and another

14.2% considered them useful while 23.8% considered them somewhat useful. Nearly half considered them not really too useful or virtually useless.

Similarly, we asked the colleges in the sample about the importance of exit interviews for graduating students. We asked them: how important were these interviews in helping you to develop and implement a retention strategy? About 9.4% said that these interviews were absolutely invaluable in developing their retention strategies and 28.1% said they were useful. Another 31.25% said they were somewhat useful, while 28.1% said they were not really too useful and 3.13% said they were virtually useless. Interestingly, it was larger colleges that consider this exercise either absolutely invaluable or useful; two-thirds of them fell into one of these two categories. For the small colleges, only about 30% fell into these two categories.

Percentage of Colleges that Maintain Records that Enable them to Pinpoint Students that do not Participate Heavily or at all in Extra-Curricular Activities

17.5% of the colleges in the sample maintain records that enabled them to pinpoint students who were not participants in any or very few extracurricular activities. Private colleges are far more likely than public colleges to keep this kind of data. Nearly 36% of the private colleges in the sample keep the data that allow them to pinpoint students who were not in any or very few extracurricular activities. Nearly 20% of the four-year or MA-granting institutions keep this kind of data, while only 14.3% of community colleges and 12.5% of PhD-granting or research universities keep it.

Information/Computer Literacy Programs a Factor in Student Retention

Information literacy has often been thought of as a key factor in retention, especially for poor students, who often come to college much less prepared than their wealthier counterparts. Many colleges have developed information literacy requirements partially aimed at addressing this imbalance, sometimes referred to as the "digital divide." We asked the colleges in the sample to characterize their information literacy efforts and to choose from the following categories. These were the choices: one: they had no specific information or computer literacy requirement; two: they teach information computer literacy within the framework of the basic English writing course; three: they require a one- or two-credit information literacy or computer literacy course to graduate; four: require one or more three-credit information literacy or computer literacy courses for graduation.

Thirty percent of the colleges in the sample said they had no specific information or computer literacy requirement. 42.5% said that they teach computer or information literacy in the framework of the basic English writing course or some other basic course. 7.5% said that they require one- or two-credit information or computer literacy courses for graduation; 20% required one or more three-credit information literacy or computer literacy courses for graduation. About 28.6% of private colleges require one or more three-credit information or computer literacy courses for graduation -- nearly twice the number of the public colleges; only 15.4% of them required one or more three-credit information literacy or computer literacy courses for graduation.

More private colleges than public colleges had no specific information or computer literacy requirement. Nearly 36% of the private colleges in the sample did not have any computer literacy or information literacy requirement of any kind, while only about 27% of the public colleges were in this category. Moreover, 46.2% of the public colleges in the sample teach information literacy within the framework of the basic English writing course or some other basic course; this was the case for only about 36% of the private colleges. In general, the tendency to require a three- or more credit course information literacy or computer literacy for graduation was inversely related to student enrollment. Only 9.1% of colleges with 10,000 or more students required a three-credit computer or information literacy course to graduate, while 20.6% of colleges with between 2,000 and 10,000 students required such a course. 28% of the colleges with less than 2,000 enrollment required such a course.

Percentage of Colleges that Offer Childcare Services

About 46.2% of the colleges in the sample offer childcare services for students with children; 72% of public colleges offer such services while no private colleges in the sample did so. The tendency to offer childcare services to students with children rose with the size of the institution. Only 21.4% of the colleges in the sample with under 2,000 FT enrollment offered childcare services, while 80% of those with more than 10,000 students did, as did about 47% of those with between 2,000 and 10,000 in FTE enrollment.

Ranking in Importance of Financial Aid

We asked the colleges in the sample to rate the importance of financial aid for success in retention. We gave them five choices: very important, important, somewhat important, infrequently important and not really important. No colleges in the sample chose infrequently important or not really important. Close to 72% of the colleges in the sample chose very important; 23.1% chose important; and 5.1% chose somewhat important. There was little difference between public colleges and private colleges. Indeed, there was little difference between colleges at different enrollment levels, although those with under 2,000 FT enrollment were perhaps the most likely to consider financial aid as a critical factor in retention. Financial aid was just as important to the community colleges as to major research universities.

Ranking in Importance of Career Services for Retention

We asked the colleges in the sample to rank the importance of career services for success in retention. We gave them five choices, the same as those listed above previously. 10.3% chose very important, while 41% chose important. 36% chose somewhat important and 10.7% said it was infrequently important; 2.6% said it was not really important.

The availability of career services was a more important factor for the public colleges than for the private colleges. About 64% of the public colleges said that career services was either a very important or important factor in retention efforts while only 7.14% of private colleges said it was very important.

Ranking in Importance of Academic Advising Services for Retention

We asked the colleges in the sample to rate the importance of academic advising services for success in retention. Once again, we gave them five choices: very important, important, somewhat important, infrequently important and not really important. Two-thirds of the colleges in the sample chose very important and 25.6% chose important. No college chose either infrequently important or not really important. Private colleges were somewhat more likely than public colleges to consider academic advising as very important; 78.6% of the private colleges consider advising to be a very important factor in retention, while only 60% of public colleges did so. In general, the smaller colleges were more likely to think of academic advising as a critical factor in retention. Nearly 86% of colleges with enrollment of under 2,000 FTE consider academic advising to be very important in retention, while only 50% of colleges with enrollment of 10,000 or greater thought so.

Ranking in Importance of Learning or Tutoring Services for Retention

We asked the colleges in the sample to rate the importance of learning services or tutoring services for success in retention. Once again we gave them the same range of choices. Close to 54% considered tutoring very important while a third considered it important. Only about 12.8% considered tutoring "somewhat important" and no college chose either infrequently important or not really important. There was no significant difference between the public and private colleges in this respect. Nor did college size significantly affect the results.

Interestingly, it was the PhD-granting and research universities that considered academic tutoring and learning centers to be most critical to retention.

Ranking in Importance of Peer Mentoring for Retention

We asked the colleges in the sample to rank the importance of peer mentoring for success in retention, once again giving the same range of choices. 12.8% considered peer mentoring very important and 41% considered it important. A third considered it somewhat important, 10.3% considered it infrequently important and 2.6% considered it not really important.

Percentage of Colleges that Identify High-Risk Students and Intervene at Defined Thresholds

About 77% of the colleges in the sample say that they identify high-risk students and then intervene at certain thresholds, such as number of classes or assignments missed, or low grade point averages. Nearly 86% of the private colleges in the sample and 72% of the public colleges identify high-risk students. Community colleges were most likely to have this policy.

Self-Assessment of College Efforts to Help At-Risk Students

We asked the colleges in the sample to choose among five descriptions of their efforts to reach out and help students at higher risk of dropping out. We gave them five choices: we don't do enough and are not really very good at what we do; two: we don't do enough and our present efforts are passable at best; three: we make a fairly considerable effort and we do as well as most; four: we make a great effort but without great results; five: we make a great effort and we have very good results. 15.4% of the colleges in the sample chose the first selection: we don't do enough and are not really very good at what we do. A third of the sample chose the second selection: we don't do enough and our present efforts are passable at best. 28.2% chose the third selection: we make a fairly considerable effort and do as well as most. Only 7.7% said: we make a great effort but without great results. 15.4% chose: we make a great effort and we had very good results.

Spending on Tutoring Services

The colleges in the sample spent a mean of $253,514 on tutoring services in the past year. Median spending was $73,150 and the range of spending went from zero to $1.5 million.

Public and private colleges spend very similar amounts on tutoring; mean spending for the public colleges in the sample was $262,820 while mean spending for the private colleges was $272,500. However, per-student spending was dramatically higher for the private colleges, which had much lower total enrollments than the public colleges in the sample. Both community colleges and PhD or research universities spend relatively modest amounts, averaging about $66,000 between them, while four-year or M.A. degree-granting institutions spend heavily on tutoring, averaging $388,562 per year.

The colleges in the sample plan to increase spending modestly on tutoring in the coming year to a mean of $279,705. Private colleges plan to increase spending significantly to a mean of $350,400, while increases for public colleges were far more modest. Their plans were to increase spending to a mean of $274,787. Once again it was the four-year or MA-degree granting institutions that plan the greatest increases. Other types of colleges plan virtually no increase whatsoever.

Rating of the Importance of Tutoring Programs in Retention

We asked the colleges in the sample to rank the impact of college tutoring programs on student retention. We gave them four choices; the first one was: I don't think tutoring can have a big impact on retention. The second one was: we need to hire more tutors, train them better, or both. Third: we have a good tutoring program that has helped us to maintain or increase our retention levels. Fourth: our tutoring program is excellent and is a key factor in our maintenance of a higher-than-expected retention level. Only 3% of the colleges in the sample chose the first choice: I don't think tutoring can have a big impact on retention. A full third chose the second choice: we need to hire more tutors, train them better, or both. More than half, 51.52%, selected the third choice: we have a good tutoring program that has helped us to maintain or increase our retention levels. 12.2% chose the fourth choice: our tutoring program is excellent and a key factor in our maintenance of a higher-than-expected retention level. The largest colleges, those with 10,000 or more FTE students, were the most enthusiastic about their tutoring programs; 22.22% of them said that their tutoring program is excellent and is a key factor in the maintenance of a higher-than-expected retention level. They say this despite the fact that they tend to spend very little on tutoring.

Level of Centralization of College Tutoring Programs

We asked the colleges in the sample to describe the level of centralization of their tutoring program. They were asked to choose one of three descriptions. The first choice was: we don't really have a formal policy of any kind. The second choice was: most tutoring is handled in a decentralized way by specific academic departments or administrative agencies. Third: most tutoring is handled through requests to a centralized college agency. Most respondents selected the third choice; 63.6% of respondents said that tutoring is handled through requests to a centralized agency and only 27.3% said it was handled in a decentralized fashion. 9.1% said they did not have a formal policy.

Payment Arrangements for Tutoring

About 76% of the colleges in the sample use students as tutors and only 6% use specialized professional tutors. For roughly 82% of the respondents in the sample, students did not pay for tutoring. For more than 15%, students pay some of the cost and at 4.3% of the colleges the sample students pay all the costs of tutoring. There was no great difference in this respect between the public and private colleges; students tend to pay some of the cost of tutoring to a greater extent at the PhD-granting or research universities than at other types of higher education institutions in the sample.

Policies Towards Tutoring Requests in the Last Three Weeks of a Semester

We asked colleges what their attitude was towards tutoring requests that come within the final three weeks of the final regular class in the semester. We gave them five choices and asked them to pick the one which best characterized their policy. The choices were: we don't really provide tutors. The second was: we have a firm cutoff date and don't take tutoring requests after this time. The third was: we have a firm cutoff date but this is later than three weeks before the final regular class. The fourth was: we don't have a tutoring cutoff date but realistically it is more difficult to meet requests this late in the semester. The last selection was: we don't have a tutoring cutoff date and are able to serve students just as well at this time as at other times in the semester. Overwhelmingly, respondents chose the last two selections, especially the fourth: we have a tutoring cutoff date but realistically it is more difficult to meet requests this late in the semester. About 58% of those sampled selected this choice. However, another 30.3% selected the final choice: we don't have a tutoring cutoff date and are able to serve students just as well this time as that any other time in the semester. Private colleges were more likely than public colleges to choose this final choice; smaller colleges were far more likely than other colleges to be able to effectively offer tutoring services in the last few weeks of the semester. Indeed, 58% of them said that they could provide tutors as well during this period as in any other and don't have a tutoring cutoff date.

Pay Rates for Student Tutors

We asked the colleges in the sample how much they were paying their student tutors. A third pay them less than $8 per hour; about 47% pay them from $8-$10 per hour. 13.33% pay them from $11-$14 per hour and 3.33% pay them from $15-$20 per hour. Only 3.33% pay them more than $20 per hour. Differences between pay levels of the public and private colleges or among the colleges of different sizes and types were not great.

Percentage of Colleges with Student Advisory Services Located in Residence Halls

9.4% of the colleges in the sample had student advisory centers located in residence halls. All the colleges that had student advisory services located in residence halls were PhD-granting or research universities.

Percentage of Colleges that have Hired a Consultant to Review or Revise the Academic Advising Unit

21.2% of the colleges in the sample had ever hired a consultant to review or advise on the College's academic advising services; these are mostly larger colleges, 50% of which have hired a consultant for this purpose

Mean Annual Budget for the Academic Advising Unit

The mean annual budget, including spending for salaries, of a college academic advising unit for the colleges in the sample was $695,626. Median spending was $380,000 with a maximum of $5 million. The public colleges spent much more than private colleges, nearly 4 times as much.

Number of Full-Time Equivalent Positions in the Academic Advising Unit

The mean number of full-time equivalent positions allocated to academic advising was approximately 14.6; public colleges employed more than 6 times as many individuals in academic advising as the private colleges did, a mean of 18.9 vs. 3.1.

Self-Assessment of Growth in Financial Aid in the Past Two Years

We asked the colleges in the sample to describe the growth of their college's financial aid over the past two years, since financial aid is such an important consideration in retention. We gave them five choices in describing their financial aid. The first choice was: it's become much less generous. The second choice was: it has become somewhat less generous. The third choice was: it has remained about the same in real terms. The fourth choice was: it has become somewhat more generous. And the fifth choice was: it has become much more generous. Most, about 55%, selected choice three: it has remained about the same in real terms. A little more than a quarter chose the fourth selection: it has become somewhat more generous. None said that it has become much more generous. 12.9% said their financial aid has become somewhat less generous and 6.45% said it had become much less generous. On the whole, 40% of private colleges in the sample said that their policies had become somewhat more generous; merely 19% of the public colleges made this choice. More than 45% of colleges with fewer than 2,000 students said that their financial aid policies had become somewhat more generous. Also, all of the community colleges in the sample said that their financial aid policies had remained the same or had become somewhat more generous in the recent past.

Evaluation of Capacity of Students to Pay for College

We also asked the colleges in the sample to comment on the capacity of their student body to pay the tuition charged at their college. We gave them three choices; the first was: it has become more and more difficult for students to pay for college. The second choice was: the overall financial burden on our students has not changed much in recent years. The third choice was: our aid programs and a strong economy have actually reduced the financial burden on our students in recent years. Only 3.23% of the colleges in the sample chose number three, that the financial burden on students has been reduced in recent years. About 35.5% said that the overall financial burden on students has not changed much in recent years, while 61.3% said it has become more difficult for students to pay for college. Interestingly, more private colleges than public colleges believed that students were facing greater difficulty in paying their tuition. While 70% of private colleges in the sample said it had become more and more difficult for students to pay for college, this was true of only 57.14% of public colleges. Among the community colleges 80% believe that the burden has not changed much on students or that it has actually been reduced in recent years. Among the four-year or MA degree-granting institutions, 75% believe that it has become more difficult for students to pay for college. This data suggests increasing pressure on private college tuitions, especially for the four-year liberal arts type colleges.

Level of Financial Aid or Tuition Reductions Needed to Maintain or Expand Enrollment

We asked the colleges in the sample what kind of changes to tuition and financial aid should be made over the next few years at their institution in order for them to retain and enhance the quality of students attracted to the institution and to maintain or increase enrollment. We gave them three choices; the first was: lower tuition, increase financial aid or both. The second choice was: do not make any serious changes in this way. The third choice was: we can increase tuition and still attract the same quality and number of students. Only about 26% of the colleges in the sample felt that they could increase tuition and still attract the same quality and number of students. About 39% felt that they do not have to make any serious changes in terms of lowering tuition or increasing financial aid or both. About

35.5% felt that their institution should lower tuition, increase financial aid or both. Half of the private colleges in the sample felt that in order to attract students at the same level of quality they would have to lower tuition increase financial aid or both. This was true of only a little more than 28.5% of the public colleges in the sample. Once again, it was a smaller colleges, those with fewer than 2,000 students, that clearly believed that they had to lower tuition or increase financial aid or both. Nearly 64% of colleges in the sample with enrollments of under 2,000 FTE believe that they would have to lower tuition, increase financial aid or both.

Policies Concerning the Encouragement of Student-Instructor Interaction Outside of the Classroom

We asked the colleges in the sample to comments on the institution's attitude towards encouraging student-instructor interaction outside of the classroom, thought to be a factor in retention by many experts. We gave them three choices; the first was: we don't really have a policy on this issue. The second was: we encourage this contact in a casual way. The third choice was: we encourage faculty to reach out to students in extracurricular work, extended office hours, attendance at off-campus events and other forms of participation with students. Nearly 55% of the colleges in the sample chose this last option, while 22.6% said they encourage contact in a casual way and about 22.6% said that they don't have a policy on this issue. There was little difference between public and private colleges over this issue and the data are nearly identical for both parties.

Percentage of the Student Body Born Abroad

We asked the colleges in the sample: what percentage of your student body was born abroad? The mean percentage of students born abroad for the colleges in the sample was 8.66%; the range was zero to 35% with a median of 4.5%. Private colleges had a slightly higher percentage of their student body born abroad, at 10.8%. In general, the larger the college in terms of enrollment, the higher the percentage of students born abroad. For those colleges with under 2,000 FTE, the mean percentage of students born abroad was 6.25%, rising to 9.73% for those colleges with between 2,000 and 10,000 students and increasing again to 12.17% for those colleges with more than 10,000 students FTE. Similarly the percentage of students born abroad increased as the complexity of degrees awarded increased. For community colleges, 7.5% of the student body was born abroad, rising to 8.86% for the four-year or MA-granting colleges and to 11.38% for the PhD-granting and/or research universities in the sample.

Special Help in Reading, Writing or Pronouncing English

We asked the colleges in the sample approximately what percentage of the students who start as freshmen or transferees at their college in the past year need special help in reading, writing or pronouncing English language in order to have a good chance at being effective college students. The mean percentage of students requiring special assistance was 27.5% with a mean of 15% and a range of zero to 85%. Public colleges encounter this difficulty nearly 3 times as often as the private colleges. Nearly 36% of students at the public colleges require special assistance compared to just 12.56% of students at the private colleges.

We asked the colleges in the sample what percentage of them offered classes in English as a second language. More than 58% did so, including more than two-thirds of the public colleges and more than 87% of colleges with enrollment levels of more than 10,000 FTE.

Recent Trends in Retention Levels

We asked the colleges in the sample what was the trend in retention levels for first-year students entering their second year. We gave them three choices; the first was: retention level had remained about the same for the past two years. The second choice was: the retention level had increased in the past two years. The third choice was: the retention level had decreased in the past two years. More than 58% of the colleges in the sample noted that they had not experienced any significant change in the retention level over the past two years; 22.58% said their retention level had increased in the past two years, while 19.35% said that it had decreased. Interestingly, more than 40% of the private colleges in the sample said that their retention levels had decreased in the past two years, more than 4 times the percentage for the public colleges, which was 9.52%. Similarly, 28.6% of the public colleges said that their retention levels have increased in the past two years, nearly 3 times the level of the private colleges, of which only 10% said that their retention levels have increased in the past two years. The experience of the largest colleges was particularly favorable. No college in the sample with enrollment of 10,000 or more students FTE experienced a decrease in retention levels in the past two years while 37.5% of them experienced an increase and 62.5% said they had remained the same.

Percentage of Dropouts Attributed to Economic Reasons

We asked the colleges in the sample what percentage of students who dropped out did so primarily for economic reasons. Overall, survey respondents estimated that 25.74% of students who dropped out did so for economic reasons. The median figure was 16.5% and the range was zero to 65%. As might be expected, public colleges had more serious problems in this way than the private colleges. About

31% of dropouts from public colleges did so primarily for economic reasons, but this is the case for only 17.43% of dropouts from private colleges.

Expectations of College Administrators for Changes in Retention Rates

We asked the colleges in the sample whether they expected retention rates to increase, decrease or remain the same. More than 58% expected retention rates to increase, and 35.5% expected retention rates to stay about the same. Only 6.45% of those sampled expected retention rates to decline. Given the current economic environment in the United States, we suspect that this includes a dose of wishful thinking. PhD-granting or research universities were the most pessimistic, with a third of those expecting declines in retention rates; these universities accounted for all of those in the sample that expected retention rates to decline.

Percentage of Colleges that Have Developed Learning Communities

We asked the colleges in the sample whether they had ever developed a learning community or group of students who take more than one class together and form a faculty assistant academic support group for one another. 40% of the colleges in the sample said they have used this tactic often; another 36.7% say they have used this tactic but not with great success. 22.33% say they have never used this tactic. It was the largest colleges that used this tactic the most and with the most success.

Chapter One: Spending On Student Retention

Table 1.1:   Mean, Median, Minimum And Maximum College Spending On Consulting Services To Aid In Student Retention In The Past Year, In US$

	Mean	Median	Minimum	Maximum
Entire Sample	25,527.03	0.00	0.00	500,000.00

Table 1.2:   Mean, Median, Minimum And Maximum College Spending On Consulting Services To Aid In Student Retention In The Past Year, In US$, Broken Out By Public/Private Status

Public/Private	Mean	Median	Minimum	Maximum
Public College	41,357.14	0.00	0.00	500,000.00
Private College	6,909.09	0.00	0.00	75,000.00

Table 1.3:   Mean, Median, Minimum And Maximum College Spending On Consulting Services To Aid In Student Retention In The Past Year, In US$, Broken Out By FTE Enrollment

FTE Enrollment	Mean	Median	Minimum	Maximum
Under 2,000 FTE Enrollment	6,818.18	0.00	0.00	75,000.00
2,000 To 10,000 FTE Enrollment	44,961.54	0.00	0.00	500.000.00
10,000+ FTE Enrollment	35,625.00	0.00	0.00	200.000.00

Table 1.4:   Mean, Median, Minimum And Maximum College Spending On Consulting Services To Aid In Student Retention In The Past Year, In US$, Broken Out By Type Of College

Type Of College	Mean	Median	Minimum	Maximum
Community College	3,916.67	0.00	0.00	17,500.00
4-Year Or MA Degree Granting Institution	32,190.48	0.00	0.00	500,000.00
PhD Granting Institution Or Research University	49,000.00	0.00	0.00	200,000.00

Table 1.5:   Mean, Median, Minimum And Maximum Projected Spending On Consulting Services To Aid In Student Retention In The Next Year

	Mean	Median	Minimum	Maximum
Entire Sample	14,027.78	0.00	0.00	275,000.00

Table 1.6:   Mean, Median, Minimum And Maximum Projected Spending On Consulting Services To Aid In Student Retention In The Next Year, Broken Out By Public/Private Status

Public/Private	Mean	Median	Minimum	Maximum
Public College	24,375.00	0.00	0.00	275,000.00
Private College	1,590.91	0.00	0.00	10,000.00

Table 1.7:   Mean, Median, Minimum And Maximum Projected Spending On Consulting Services To Aid In Student Retention In The Next Year, Broken Out By FTE Enrollment

FTE Enrollment	Mean	Median	Minimum	Maximum
Under 2,000 FTE Enrollment	227.27	0.00	0.00	2,500.00
2,000 To 10,000 FTE Enrollment	14,791.67	7,000.00	0.00	100,000.00
10,000+ FTE Enrollment	40,625.00	0.00	0.00	275,000.00

Table 1.8:   Mean, Median, Minimum And Maximum Projected Spending On Consulting Services To Aid In Student Retention In The Next Year, Broken Out By Type Of College

Type Of College	Mean	Median	Minimum	Maximum
Community College	3,583.33	0.00	0.00	12,500.00
4-Year Or MA Degree Granting Institution	9,425.00	0.00	0.00	100,000.00
PhD Granting Institution Or Research University	59,000.00	0.00	0.00	275,000.00

Table 1.9:   Mean, Median, Minimum And Maximum Approximate College Spending On Conferences, Webcasts, Research Reports And Other Specialized Publications About Student Retention In The Past Year

	Mean	Median	Minimum	Maximum
Entire Sample	9,696.15	2,000.00	0.00	100,000.00

Table 1.10: Mean, Median, Minimum And Maximum Approximate College Spending On Conferences, Webcasts, Research Reports And Other Specialized Publications About Student Retention In The Past Year, Broken Out By Public/Private Status

Public/Private	Mean	Median	Minimum	Maximum
Public College	15,028.57	5,500.00	500.00	100,000.00
Private College	5,212.50	1,000.00	0.00	36,000.00

Table 1.11: Mean, Median, Minimum And Maximum Approximate College Spending On Conferences, Webcasts, Research Reports And Other Specialized Publications About Student Retention In The Past Year, Broken Out By FTE Enrollment

FTE Enrollment	Mean	Median	Minimum	Maximum
Under 2,000 FTE Enrollment	5,545.83	1,000.00	0.00	36,000.00
2,000 To 10,000 FTE Enrollment	7,700.00	4,000.00	500.00	26,000.00
10,000+ FTE Enrollment	26,437.50	12,500.00	1,000.00	100,000.00

Table 1.12: Mean, Median, Minimum And Maximum Approximate College Spending On Conferences, Webcasts, Research Reports And Other Specialized Publications About Student Retention In The Past Year, Broken Out By Type Of College

Type Of College	Mean	Median	Minimum	Maximum
Community College	6,933.33	2,550.00	500.00	25,000.00
4-Year Or MA Degree Granting Institution	8,206.82	3,000.00	0.00	50,000.00
PhD Granting Institution Or Research University	31,200.00	15,000.00	5,000.00	100,000.00

Table 1.13: Percentage Of Colleges That Have A Dean Or Other High Level Administrator Whose Primary Responsibility Is To Maintain Or Increase Student Retention

	Yes	No
Entire Sample	65.00%	35.00%

Table 1.14:   Percentage Of Colleges That Have A Dean Or Other High Level Administrator Whose Primary Responsibility Is To Maintain Or Increase Student Retention, Broken Out By Public/Private Status

Public/Private	Yes	No
Public College	61.54%	38.46%
Private College	71.43%	28.57%

Table 1.15:   Percentage Of Colleges That Have A Dean Or Other High Level Administrator Whose Primary Responsibility Is To Maintain Or Increase Student Retention, Broken Out By FTE Enrollment

FTE Enrollment	Yes	No
Under 2,000 FTE Enrollment	50.00%	50.00%
2,000 To 10,000 FTE Enrollment	80.00%	20.00%
10,000+ FTE Enrollment	63.64%	36.36%

Table 1.16:   Percentage Of Colleges That Have A Dean Or Other High Level Administrator Whose Primary Responsibility Is To Maintain Or Increase Student Retention, Broken Out By Type Of College

Type Of College	Yes	No
Community College	71.43%	28.57%
4-Year Or MA Degree Granting Institution	56.00%	44.00%
PhD Granting Institution Or Research University	87.50%	12.50%

Table 1.17:   Mean, Median, Minimum And Maximum College Fall To Fall Retention Rate For First Year Students In The Fall 2006 To Fall 2007 School Year

	Mean	Median	Minimum	Maximum
Entire Sample	73.81	74.00	45.00	98.00

Table 1.18:   Mean, Median, Minimum And Maximum College Fall To Fall Retention Rate For First Year Students In The Fall 2006 To Fall 2007 School Year, Broken Out By Public/Private Status

Public/Private	Mean	Median	Minimum	Maximum
Public College	74.40	79.50	45.00	94.00
Private College	72.82	72.10	58.00	98.00

Table 1.19:   Mean, Median, Minimum And Maximum College Fall To Fall Retention Rate For First Year Students In The Fall 2006 To Fall 2007 School Year, Broken Out By FTE Enrollment

FTE Enrollment	Mean	Median	Minimum	Maximum
Under 2,000 FTE Enrollment	68.92	70.05	45.00	93.00
2,000 To 10,000 FTE Enrollment	70.21	69.00	45.00	98.00
10,000+ FTE Enrollment	82.84	82.20	71.00	94.00

Table 1.20:   Mean, Median, Minimum And Maximum College Fall To Fall Retention Rate For First Year Students In The Fall 2006 To Fall 2007 School Year, Broken Out By Type Of College

Type Of College	Mean	Median	Minimum	Maximum
Community College	71.67	70.00	65.00	80.00
4-Year Or MA Degree Granting Institution	70.72	71.55	45.00	94.00
PhD Granting Institution Or Research University	83.90	82.10	78.00	98.00

Table 1.21:   Mean, Median, Minimum And Maximum College Fall To Fall Retention Rate For Part Time Students From Fall 2006 To Fall 2007

	Mean	Median	Minimum	Maximum
Entire Sample	67.68	74.00	35.00	94.00

Table 1.22:   Mean, Median, Minimum And College Fall To Fall Retention Rate For Part Time Students From Fall 2006 To Fall 2007, Broken Out By Public/Private Status

Public/Private	Mean	Median	Minimum	Maximum
Public College	62.81	68.00	35.00	85.00
Private College	92.00	92.00	90.00	94.00

Table 1.23:   Mean, Median, Minimum And Maximum College Fall To Fall Retention Rate For Part Time Students From Fall 2006 To Fall 2007, Broken Out By FTE Enrollment

FTE Enrollment	Mean	Median	Minimum	Maximum
Under 2,000 FTE Enrollment	67.50	67.50	45.00	90.00
2,000 To 10,000 FTE Enrollment	62.00	64.00	35.00	94.00
10,000+ FTE Enrollment	73.42	78.00	47.00	85.00

Table 1.24:   Mean, Median, Minimum And Maximum College Fall To Fall Retention Rate For Part Time Students From Fall 2006 To Fall 2007, Broken Out By Type Of College

Type Of College	Mean	Median	Minimum	Maximum
Community College	45.00	45.00	45.00	45.00
4-Year Or MA Degree Granting Institution	64.33	68.00	35.00	90.00
PhD Granting Institution Or Research University	84.03	83.05	76.00	94.00

Table 1.25:   Mean, Median, Minimum And Maximum Percentage Of Students Who Start At The College As Fall Term Freshmen That Go On To Graduate

	Mean	Median	Minimum	Maximum
Entire Sample	50.99	52.50	0.00	92.00

Table 1.26:   Mean, Median, Minimum And Maximum Percentage Of Students Who Start At The College As Fall Term Freshmen That Go On To Graduate, Broken Out By Public/Private Status

Public/Private	Mean	Median	Minimum	Maximum
Public College	49.53	50.00	10.00	92.00
Private College	57.03	57.70	30.00	90.00

Table 1.27:   Mean, Median, Minimum And Maximum Percentage Of Students Who Start At The College As Fall Term Freshmen That Go On To Graduate, Broken Out By FTE Enrollment

FTE Enrollment	Mean	Median	Minimum	Maximum
Under 2,000 FTE Enrollment	51.05	50.00	10.00	89.00
2,000 To 10,000 FTE Enrollment	46.39	40.50	18.00	90.00
10,000+ FTE Enrollment	62.44	61.50	37.00	92.00

Table 1.28:   Mean, Median, Minimum And Maximum Percentage Of Students Who Start At The College As Fall Term Freshmen That Go On To Graduate, Broken Out By Type Of College

Type Of College	Mean	Median	Minimum	Maximum
Community College	50.74	61.70	15.00	73.00
4-Year Or MA Degree Granting Institution	50.39	47.00	10.00	92.00
PhD Granting Institution Or Research University	60.57	55.00	46.00	90.00

Table 1.29:   Percentage Of Colleges That Track Retention Rates By Declared Academic Major

	Yes	No
Entire Sample	65.00%	35.00%

Table 1.30:   Percentage Of Colleges That Track Retention Rates By Declared Academic Major, Broken Out By Public/Private Status

Public/Private	Yes	No
Public College	73.08%	26.92%
Private College	50.00%	50.00%

Table 1.31:   Percentage Of Colleges That Track Retention Rates By Declared Academic Major, Broken Out By FTE Enrollment

FTE Enrollment	Yes	No
Under 2,000 FTE Enrollment	50.00%	50.00%
2,000 To 10,000 FTE Enrollment	73.33%	26.67%
10,000+ FTE Enrollment	72.73%	27.27%

Table 1.32:   Percentage Of Colleges That Track Retention Rates By Declared Academic Major, Broken Out By Type Of College

Type Of College	Yes	No
Community College	85.71%	14.29%
4-Year Or MA Degree Granting Institution	60.00%	40.00%
PhD Granting Institution Or Research University	62.50%	37.50%

Table 1.33:   Percentage Of Colleges That Track Retention Rates By Grade Point Average Or SAT Level

	Yes	No
Entire Sample	42.50%	57.50%

Table 1.34:   Percentage Of Colleges That Track Retention Rates By Grade Point Average Or SAT Level, Broken Out By Public/Private Status

Public/Private	Yes	No
Public College	42.31%	57.69%
Private College	42.86%	57.14%

Table 1.35:   Percentage Of Colleges That Track Retention Rates By Grade Point Average Or SAT Level, Broken Out By FTE Enrollment

FTE Enrollment	Yes	No
Under 2,000 FTE Enrollment	35.71%	64.29%
2,000 To 10,000 FTE Enrollment	46.67%	53.33%
10,000+ FTE Enrollment	45.45%	54.55%

Table 1.36:   Percentage Of Colleges That Track Retention Rates By Grade Point Average Or SAT Level, Broken Out By Type Of College

Type Of College	Yes	No
Community College	14.29%	85.71%
4-Year Or MA Degree Granting Institution	44.00%	56.00%
PhD Granting Institution Or Research University	62.50%	37.50%

Table 1.37:   Percentage Of Colleges That Track Retention Rates By Gender

	Yes	No
Entire Sample	65.00%	35.00%

Table 1.38:   Percentage Of Colleges That Track Retention Rates By Gender, Broken Out By Public/Private Status

Public/Private	Yes	No
Public College	61.54%	38.46%
Private College	71.43%	28.57%

Table 1.39:   Percentage Of Colleges That Track Retention Rates By Gender, Broken Out By FTE Enrollment

FTE Enrollment	Yes	No
Under 2,000 FTE Enrollment	50.00%	50.00%
2,000 To 10,000 FTE Enrollment	66.67%	33.33%
10,000+ FTE Enrollment	81.82%	18.18%

Table 1.40:   Percentage Of Colleges That Track Retention Rates By Gender, Broken Out By Type Of College

Type Of College	Yes	No
Community College	14.29%	85.71%
4-Year Or MA Degree Granting Institution	72.00%	28.00%
PhD Granting Institution Or Research University	87.50%	12.50%

Table 1.41:   Percentage Of Colleges That Track Retention Rates By Race

	Yes	No
Entire Sample	75.00%	25.00%

Table 1.42:   Percentage Of Colleges That Track Retention Rates By Race, Broken Out By Public/Private Status

Public/Private	Yes	No
Public College	69.23%	30.77%
Private College	85.71%	14.29%

Table 1.43:   Percentage Of Colleges That Track Retention Rates By Race, Broken Out By FTE Enrollment

FTE Enrollment	Yes	No
Under 2,000 FTE Enrollment	64.29%	35.71%
2,000 To 10,000 FTE Enrollment	73.33%	26.67%
10,000+ FTE Enrollment	90.91%	9.09%

Table 1.44: Percentage Of Colleges That Track Retention Rates By Race, Broken Out By Type Of College

Type Of College	Yes	No
Community College	28.57%	71.43%
4-Year Or MA Degree Granting Institution	80.00%	20.00%
PhD Granting Institution Or Research University	100.00%	0.00%

Table 1.45: Percentage Of Colleges That Track Retention Rates For Transferees Into College

	Yes	No
Entire Sample	47.50%	52.50%

Table 1.46: Percentage Of Colleges That Track Retention Rates For Transferees Into College, Broken Out By Public/Private Status

Public/Private	Yes	No
Public College	53.85%	46.15%
Private College	35.71%	64.29%

Table 1.47: Percentage Of Colleges That Track Retention Rates For Transferees Into College, Broken Out By FTE Enrollment

FTE Enrollment	Yes	No
Under 2,000 FTE Enrollment	35.71%	64.29%
2,000 To 10,000 FTE Enrollment	53.33%	46.67%
10,000+ FTE Enrollment	54.55%	45.45%

Table 1.48: Percentage Of Colleges That Track Retention Rates For Transferees Into College, Broken Out By Type Of College

Type Of College	Yes	No
Community College	28.57%	71.43%
4-Year Or MA Degree Granting Institution	52.00%	48.00%
PhD Granting Institution Or Research University	50.00%	50.00%

Survey of Student Retention Policies in Higher Education

We asked the sample if they have had particular success in increasing retention rates for any specific group defined by any criteria (race, SAT level, academic major, geographic origin, or any other criteria) and to explain how they achieved this success.

1. University college program (freshman students who are specially admitted students have higher retention rates than the remaining freshmen who were classified as regular admits). UCP requires students to enroll in freshman seminar courses, intrusive advising, academic monitoring, tutoring services, etc.
2. Designated peer mentors, frequent contact, early alert, frequent meetings.
3. Implemented a Native American learning community.
4. Learning disabilities program.
5. Focusing on establishing a mentoring program for students who are not connected on campus through residence halls, scholarship programs, etc. Primary focus on students of color. We have not seen final assessment on this program, which was piloted this fall (2007).
6. Majors in the school of agriculture, fisheries and human sciences have a higher retention rate. There are special programs and retention initiatives in place for those majors.
7. Minorities and males who are involved in athletics have higher graduation rates at our college
8. Intrusive advising.
9. Started a student success center, emphasized retention committee, engaged in lots of research, recruited better first-year students.
10. Smaller communities based upon some racial identity, but mainly first generation and income status--peer mentoring and intrusive counseling techniques.
11. Currently doing analysis of race, first-generation students & undergrad major, so no statistics available yet. However, we have been successful with peer and faculty mentorship programs and having a full-time learning specialist specifically for the dental students.
12. Making placement testing and implementation mandatory.
13. We are now just implementing a campus-wide retention initiative.
14. Intensive tracking, sharing information about at-risk students with deans and senior administrators, term-by-term tracking of each cohort.
15. Student retention rates in our EOF program are significantly higher due to the advising model employed. Assigning advisors and increasing faculty advising have assisted increasing student retention.
16. We are an open-admission, urban institution. The development of a comprehensive center for student progress provides intensive support for all students from orientation through graduation. The center provides orientation services, first-year student services, individual intervention services, multicultural student services, adult learner services, student tutorial services, supplemental instruction services and disability services. All services are interconnected with excellent support staff. Outreach to students is front-loaded and pleasantly proactive. Since connections begin at orientation, center use is normalized for all students: at-risk to highly competitive. Please see our Website for more comprehensive information at www.cc.ysu.edu/csp/.
17. Our numbers are so small it is hard to tell.
18. We instituted living-learning communities for first-year students in 2005, and the retention rate for participants vs. non-participants has increased. We also introduced a student life initiative in 2005 that brought more out-of-class activity to campus, and feel that this has had an indirect (if not direct) impact on retention.
19. Most of our success with freshmen has been due to our first-year experience program.

Chapter Two: Perception Of Critical Factors In Retention

Table 2.1:   Impact Of The Terms Of Student Financial Assistance On Student Retention

	Does Not Have Much Of An Impact	Has Some Impact	Has A Significant Impact	Has A Dramatic Impact
Entire Sample	5.00%	20.00%	42.50%	32.50%

Table 2.2:   Impact Of The Terms Of Student Financial Assistance On Student Retention, Broken Out By Public/Private Status

Public/Private	Does Not Have Much Of An Impact	Has Some Impact	Has A Significant Impact	Has A Dramatic Impact
Public College	7.69%	15.38%	50.00%	26.92%
Private College	0.00%	28.57%	28.57%	42.86%

Table 2.3:   Impact Of The Terms Of Student Financial Assistance On Student Retention, Broken Out By FTE Enrollment

FTE Enrollment	Does Not Have Much Of An Impact	Has Some Impact	Has A Significant Impact	Has A Dramatic Impact
Under 2,000 FTE Enrollment	7.14%	21.43%	50.00%	21.43%
2,000 To 10,000 FTE Enrollment	6.67%	13.33%	33.33%	46.67%
10,000+ FTE Enrollment	0.00%	27.27%	45.45%	27.27%

Table 2.4:   Impact Of The Terms Of Student Financial Assistance On Student Retention, Broken Out By Type Of College

Type Of College	Does Not Have Much Of An Impact	Has Some Impact	Has A Significant Impact	Has A Dramatic Impact
Community College	28.57%	14.29%	42.86%	14.29%
4-Year Or MA Degree Granting Institution	0.00%	28.00%	36.00%	36.00%
PhD Granting Institution Or Research University	0.00%	0.00%	62.50%	37.50%

Table 2.5:   Impact Of The Severity In Grading On Student Retention

	Does Not Have Much Of An Impact	Has Some Impact	Has A Significant Impact	Has A Dramatic Impact
Entire Sample	17.50%	55.00%	20.00%	7.50%

Table 2.6:   Impact Of The Severity In Grading On Student Retention, Broken Out By Public/Private Status

Public/Private	Does Not Have Much Of An Impact	Has Some Impact	Has A Significant Impact	Has A Dramatic Impact
Public College	7.69%	57.69%	26.92%	7.69%
Private College	35.71%	50.00%	7.14%	7.14%

Table 2.7:   Impact Of The Severity In Grading On Student Retention, Broken Out By FTE Enrollment

FTE Enrollment	Does Not Have Much Of An Impact	Has Some Impact	Has A Significant Impact	Has A Dramatic Impact
Under 2,000 FTE Enrollment	21.43%	64.29%	0.00%	14.29%
2,000 To 10,000 FTE Enrollment	26.67%	40.00%	26.67%	6.67%
10,000+ FTE Enrollment	0.00%	63.64%	36.36%	0.00%

Table 2.8:   Impact Of The Severity In Grading On Student Retention, Broken Out By Type Of College

Type Of College	Does Not Have Much Of An Impact	Has Some Impact	Has A Significant Impact	Has A Dramatic Impact
Community College	28.57%	57.14%	0.00%	14.29%
4-Year Or MA Degree Granting Institution	20.00%	48.00%	24.00%	8.00%
PhD Granting Institution Or Research University	0.00%	75.00%	25.00%	0.00%

Table 2.9:   Impact Of Access To Tutoring Services On Student Retention

	Does Not Have Much Of An Impact	Has Some Impact	Has A Significant Impact	Has A Dramatic Impact
Entire Sample	17.50%	32.50%	37.50%	12.50%

Table 2.10:   Impact Of Access To Tutoring Services On Student Retention, Broken Out By Public/Private Status

Public/Private	Does Not Have Much Of An Impact	Has Some Impact	Has A Significant Impact	Has A Dramatic Impact
Public College	3.85%	34.62%	42.31%	19.23%
Private College	42.86%	28.57%	28.57%	0.00%

Table 2.11:   Impact Of Access To Tutoring Services On Student Retention, Broken Out By FTE Enrollment

FTE Enrollment	Does Not Have Much Of An Impact	Has Some Impact	Has A Significant Impact	Has A Dramatic Impact
Under 2,000 FTE Enrollment	35.71%	42.86%	14.29%	7.14%
2,000 To 10,000 FTE Enrollment	13.33%	33.33%	33.33%	20.00%
10,000+ FTE Enrollment	0.00%	18.18%	72.73%	9.09%

Table 2.12:   Impact Of Access To Tutoring Services On Student Retention, Broken Out By Type Of College

Type Of College	Does Not Have Much Of An Impact	Has Some Impact	Has A Significant Impact	Has A Dramatic Impact
Community College	0.00%	57.14%	14.29%	28.57%
4-Year Or MA Degree Granting Institution	28.00%	28.00%	36.00%	8.00%
PhD Granting Institution Or Research University	0.00%	25.00%	62.50%	12.50%

Table 2.13: Impact Of Access To Academic And/Or Psychological Counseling Services On Student Retention

	Does Not Have Much Of An Impact	Has Some Impact	Has A Significant Impact	Has A Dramatic Impact
Entire Sample	10.00%	40.00%	35.00%	15.00%

Table 2.14: Impact Of Access To Academic And/Or Psychological Counseling Services On Student Retention, Broken Out By Public/Private Status

Public/Private	Does Not Have Much Of An Impact	Has Some Impact	Has A Significant Impact	Has A Dramatic Impact
Public College	7.69%	34.62%	42.31%	15.38%
Private College	14.29%	50.00%	21.43%	14.29%

Table 2.15: Impact Of Access To Academic And/Or Psychological Counseling Services On Student Retention, Broken Out By FTE Enrollment

FTE Enrollment	Does Not Have Much Of An Impact	Has Some Impact	Has A Significant Impact	Has A Dramatic Impact
Under 2,000 FTE Enrollment	14.29%	64.29%	21.43%	0.00%
2,000 To 10,000 FTE Enrollment	6.67%	40.00%	26.67%	26.67%
10,000+ FTE Enrollment	9.09%	9.09%	63.64%	18.18%

Table 2.16: Impact Of Access To Academic And/Or Psychological Counseling Services On Student Retention, Broken Out By Type Of College

Type Of College	Does Not Have Much Of An Impact	Has Some Impact	Has A Significant Impact	Has A Dramatic Impact
Community College	0.00%	57.14%	28.57%	14.29%
4-Year Or MA Degree Granting Institution	16.00%	40.00%	36.00%	8.00%
PhD Granting Institution Or Research University	0.00%	25.00%	37.50%	37.50%

Table 2.17: Impact Of General Economic Conditions On Student Retention

	Does Not Have Much Of An Impact	Has Some Impact	Has A Significant Impact	Has A Dramatic Impact
Entire Sample	10.00%	42.50%	27.50%	20.00%

Table 2.18: Impact Of General Economic Conditions On Student Retention, Broken Out By Public/Private Status

Public/Private	Does Not Have Much Of An Impact	Has Some Impact	Has A Significant Impact	Has A Dramatic Impact
Public College	7.69%	38.46%	30.77%	23.08%
Private College	14.29%	50.00%	21.43%	14.29%

Table 2.19: Impact Of General Economic Conditions On Student Retention, Broken Out By FTE Enrollment

FTE Enrollment	Does Not Have Much Of An Impact	Has Some Impact	Has A Significant Impact	Has A Dramatic Impact
Under 2,000 FTE Enrollment	14.29%	42.86%	21.43%	21.43%
2,000 To 10,000 FTE Enrollment	6.67%	33.33%	26.67%	33.33%
10,000+ FTE Enrollment	9.09%	54.55%	36.36%	0.00%

Table 2.20: Impact Of General Economic Conditions On Student Retention, Broken Out By Type Of College

Type Of College	Does Not Have Much Of An Impact	Has Some Impact	Has A Significant Impact	Has A Dramatic Impact
Community College	14.29%	0.00%	42.86%	42.86%
4-Year Or MA Degree Granting Institution	12.00%	56.00%	16.00%	16.00%
PhD Granting Institution Or Research University	0.00%	37.50%	50.00%	12.50%

Table 2.21:   Impact Of Involvement In Extra Curricular Activities On Student Retention

	Does Not Have Much Of An Impact	Has Some Impact	Has A Significant Impact	Has A Dramatic Impact
Entire Sample	10.00%	42.50%	30.00%	17.50%

Table 2.22:   Impact Of Involvement In Extra Curricular Activities On Student Retention, Broken Out By Public/Private Status

Public/Private	Does Not Have Much Of An Impact	Has Some Impact	Has A Significant Impact	Has A Dramatic Impact
Public College	11.54%	50.00%	23.08%	15.38%
Private College	7.14%	28.57%	42.86%	21.43%

Table 2.23:   Impact Of Involvement In Extra Curricular Activities On Student Retention, Broken Out By FTE Enrollment

FTE Enrollment	Does Not Have Much Of An Impact	Has Some Impact	Has A Significant Impact	Has A Dramatic Impact
Under 2,000 FTE Enrollment	21.43%	28.57%	21.43%	28.57%
2,000 To 10,000 FTE Enrollment	6.67%	46.67%	33.33%	13.33%
10,000+ FTE Enrollment	0.00%	54.55%	36.36%	9.09%

Table 2.24:   Impact Of Involvement In Extra Curricular Activities On Student Retention, Broken Out By Type Of College

Type Of College	Does Not Have Much Of An Impact	Has Some Impact	Has A Significant Impact	Has A Dramatic Impact
Community College	42.86%	14.29%	28.57%	14.29%
4-Year Or MA Degree Granting Institution	4.00%	48.00%	24.00%	24.00%
PhD Granting Institution Or Research University	0.00%	50.00%	50.00%	0.00%

Table 2.25:   Impact Of Quality Of Residence Halls And Food Service On Student Retention

	Does Not Have Much Of An Impact	Has Some Impact	Has A Significant Impact	Has A Dramatic Impact
Entire Sample	42.50%	37.50%	12.50%	7.50%

Table 2.26:   Impact Of Quality Of Residence Halls And Food Service On Student Retention, Broken Out By Public/Private Status

Public/Private	Does Not Have Much Of An Impact	Has Some Impact	Has A Significant Impact	Has A Dramatic Impact
Public College	50.00%	34.62%	7.69%	7.69%
Private College	28.57%	42.86%	21.43%	7.14%

Table 2.27:   Impact Of Quality Of Residence Halls And Food Service On Student Retention, Broken Out By FTE Enrollment

FTE Enrollment	Does Not Have Much Of An Impact	Has Some Impact	Has A Significant Impact	Has A Dramatic Impact
Under 2,000 FTE Enrollment	57.14%	28.57%	7.14%	7.14%
2,000 To 10,000 FTE Enrollment	33.33%	40.00%	13.33%	13.33%
10,000+ FTE Enrollment	36.36%	45.45%	18.18%	0.00%

Table 2.28:   Impact Of Quality Of Residence Halls And Food Service On Student Retention, Broken Out By Type Of College

Type Of College	Does Not Have Much Of An Impact	Has Some Impact	Has A Significant Impact	Has A Dramatic Impact
Community College	100.00%	0.00%	0.00%	0.00%
4-Year Or MA Degree Granting Institution	32.00%	44.00%	12.00%	12.00%
PhD Granting Institution Or Research University	25.00%	50.00%	25.00%	0.00%

Chapter Three: Student Exit Interviews

Table 3.1:   Mean, Median, Minimum And Maximum Approximate Percentage Of Students Who Decide To Transfer Out Of Or Drop Out Of The College Prior To Graduation That Are Interviewed By College Management To Find Out Their Feelings About Their Experience At The College

	Mean	Median	Minimum	Maximum
Entire Sample	26.11	5.00	0.00	100.00

Table 3.2:   Mean, Median, Minimum And Maximum Approximate Percentage Of Students Who Decide To Transfer Out Of Or Drop Out Of The College Prior To Graduation That Are Interviewed By College Management To Find Out Their Feelings About Their Experience At The College, Broken Out By Public/Private Status

Public/Private	Mean	Median	Minimum	Maximum
Public College	16.57	1.00	0.00	100.00
Private College	41.79	37.50	0.00	100.00

Table 3.3:   Mean, Median, Minimum And Maximum Approximate Percentage Of Students Who Decide To Transfer Out Of Or Drop Out Of The College Prior To Graduation That Are Interviewed By College Management To Find Out Their Feelings About Their Experience At The College, Broken Out By FTE Enrollment

FTE Enrollment	Mean	Median	Minimum	Maximum
Under 2,000 FTE Enrollment	38.08	25.00	0.00	95.00
2,000 To 10,000 FTE Enrollment	25.57	7.50	0.00	100.00
10,000+ FTE Enrollment	11.30	1.00	0.00	100.00

Table 3.4:   Mean, Median, Minimum And Maximum Approximate Percentage Of Students Who Decide To Transfer Out Of Or Drop Out Of The College Prior To Graduation That Are Interviewed By College Management To Find Out Their Feelings About Their Experience At The College, Broken Out By Type Of College

Type Of College	Mean	Median	Minimum	Maximum
Community College	22.14	5.00	0.00	100.00
4-Year Or MA Degree Granting Institution	25.17	10.00	0.00	95.00
PhD Granting Institution Or Research University	34.50	3.00	0.00	100.00

Table 3.5:   Mean, Median, Minimum And Maximum Approximate Percentage Of Students Who Graduate The College That Are Interviewed By College Management To Find Out Their Feelings About Their Experience At The College

	Mean	Median	Minimum	Maximum
Entire Sample	34.06	15.00	0.00	100.00

Table 3.6:   Mean, Median, Minimum And Maximum Approximate Percentage Of Students Who Graduate The College That Are Interviewed By College Management To Find Out Their Feelings About Their Experience At The College, Broken Out By Public/Private Status

Public/Private	Mean	Median	Minimum	Maximum
Public College	33.00	12.00	0.00	100.00
Private College	35.64	27.50	0.00	100.00

Table 3.7:   Mean, Median, Minimum And Maximum Approximate Percentage Of Students Who Graduate The College That Are Interviewed By College Management To Find Out Their Feelings About Their Experience At The College, Broken Out By FTE Enrollment

FTE Enrollment	Mean	Median	Minimum	Maximum
Under 2,000 FTE Enrollment	37.15	25.00	5.00	100.00
2,000 To 10,000 FTE Enrollment	35.87	12.00	0.00	100.00
10,000+ FTE Enrollment	24.43	5.00	0.00	100.00

Table 3.8:   Mean, Median, Minimum And Maximum Approximate Percentage Of Students Who Graduate The College That Are Interviewed By College Management To Find Out Their Feelings About Their Experience At The College, Broken Out By Type Of College

Type Of College	Mean	Median	Minimum	Maximum
Community College	44.29	30.00	5.00	100.00
4-Year Or MA Degree Granting Institution	30.75	12.50	0.00	100.00
PhD Granting Institution Or Research University	36.00	25.50	1.00	92.00

Table 3.9:   Importance Of Exit Interviews of Departing Students Who Did Not Graduate In Developing And Implementing A Retention Strategy

	Absolutely Invaluable	Useful	Somewhat Useful	Not Really Too Useful	Virtually Useless
Entire Sample	18.18%	18.18%	30.30%	24.24%	9.09%

Table 3.10:   Importance Of Exit Interviews of Departing Students Who Did Not Graduate In Developing And Implementing A Retention Strategy, Broken Out By Public/Private Status

Public/Private	Absolutely Invaluable	Useful	Somewhat Useful	Not Really Too Useful	Virtually Useless
Public College	14.29%	14.29%	23.81%	38.10%	9.52%
Private College	25.00%	25.00%	41.67%	0.00%	8.33%

Table 3.11:   Importance Of Exit Interviews of Departing Students Who Did Not Graduate In Developing And Implementing A Retention Strategy, Broken Out By FTE Enrollment

FTE Enrollment	Absolutely Invaluable	Useful	Somewhat Useful	Not Really Too Useful	Virtually Useless
Under 2,000 FTE Enrollment	25.00%	16.67%	33.33%	25.00%	0.00%
2,000 To 10,000 FTE Enrollment	14.29%	21.43%	21.43%	28.57%	14.29%
10,000+ FTE Enrollment	14.29%	14.29%	42.86%	14.29%	14.29%

Table 3.12:   Importance Of Exit Interviews of Departing Students Who Did Not Graduate In Developing And Implementing A Retention Strategy, Broken Out By Type Of College

Type Of College	Absolutely Invaluable	Useful	Somewhat Useful	Not Really Too Useful	Virtually Useless
Community College	0.00%	16.67%	33.33%	50.00%	0.00%
4-Year Or MA Degree Granting Institution	26.32%	15.79%	31.58%	21.05%	5.26%
PhD Granting Institution Or Research University	12.50%	25.00%	25.00%	12.50%	25.00%

Table 3.13:   Importance Of Exit Interviews of Graduating Students In Developing And Implementing A Retention Strategy

	Absolutely Invaluable	Useful	Somewhat Useful	Not Really Too Useful	Virtually Useless
Entire Sample	9.38%	28.13%	31.25%	28.13%	3.13%

Table 3.14:   Importance Of Exit Interviews of Graduating Students In Developing And Implementing A Retention Strategy, Broken Out By Public/Private Status

Public/Private	Absolutely Invaluable	Useful	Somewhat Useful	Not Really Too Useful	Virtually Useless
Public College	14.29%	19.05%	33.33%	33.33%	0.00%
Private College	0.00%	45.45%	27.27%	18.18%	9.09%

Table 3.15:   Importance Of Exit Interviews of Graduating Students In Developing And Implementing A Retention Strategy, Broken Out By FTE Enrollment

FTE Enrollment	Absolutely Invaluable	Useful	Somewhat Useful	Not Really Too Useful	Virtually Useless
Under 2,000 FTE Enrollment	0.00%	30.77%	38.46%	30.77%	0.00%
2,000 To 10,000 FTE Enrollment	7.69%	23.08%	30.77%	30.77%	7.69%
10,000+ FTE Enrollment	33.33%	33.33%	16.67%	16.67%	0.00%

Table 3.16:   Importance Of Exit Interviews of Graduating Students In Developing And Implementing A Retention Strategy, Broken Out By Type Of College

Type Of College	Absolutely Invaluable	Useful	Somewhat Useful	Not Really Too Useful	Virtually Useless
Community College	0.00%	14.29%	57.14%	28.57%	0.00%
4-Year Or MA Degree Granting Institution	11.11%	27.78%	22.22%	33.33%	5.56%
PhD Granting Institution Or Research University	14.29%	42.86%	28.57%	14.29%	0.00%

Chapter Four: Maximizing Student Participation In College Life

Table 4.1: Percentage Of Colleges That Maintain Any Records That Enable Them To Pinpoint Students Who Are Not Engaged In Any Or Very Few Extra-Curricular Activities

	Yes	No
Entire Sample	17.50%	82.50%

Table 4.2: Percentage Of Colleges That Maintain Any Records That Enable Them To Pinpoint Students Who Are Not Engaged In Any Or Very Few Extra-Curricular Activities, Broken Out By Public/Private Status

Public/Private	Yes	No
Public College	7.69%	92.31%
Private College	35.71%	64.29%

Table 4.3: Percentage Of Colleges That Maintain Any Records That Enable Them To Pinpoint Students Who Are Not Engaged In Any Or Very Few Extra-Curricular Activities, Broken Out By FTE Enrollment

FTE Enrollment	Yes	No
Under 2,000 FTE Enrollment	21.43%	78.57%
2,000 To 10,000 FTE Enrollment	20.00%	80.00%
10,000+ FTE Enrollment	9.09%	90.91%

Table 4.4: Percentage Of Colleges That Maintain Any Records That Enable Them To Pinpoint Students Who Are Not Engaged In Any Or Very Few Extra-Curricular Activities, Broken Out By Type Of College

Type Of College	Yes	No
Community College	14.29%	85.71%
4-Year Or MA Degree Granting Institution	20.00%	80.00%
PhD Granting Institution Or Research University	12.50%	87.50%

Chapter Five: The Basic Essential Courses

Table 5.1: Description Of College's Information Literacy Policy

	No Specific Information Or Computer Literacy Requirement	Teaches Information/Computer Literacy Within The Framework Of The Basic English Writing Course Or Other Basic Course	Requires A One Or Two Credit Information Literacy Or Computer Literacy Course For Graduation	Requires One Or More Three Credit Information Literacy Or Computer Literacy Course For Graduation
	30.00%	42.50%	7.50%	20.00%

Table 5.2: Description Of College's Information Literacy Policy, Broken Out By Public/Private Status

Public/Private	No Specific Information Or Computer Literacy Requirement	Teaches Information/Computer Literacy Within The Framework Of The Basic English Writing Course Or Other Basic Course	Requires A One Or Two Credit Information Literacy Or Computer Literacy Course For Graduation	Requires One Or More Three Credit Information Literacy Or Computer Literacy Course For Graduation
Public College	26.92%	46.15%	11.54%	15.38%
Private College	35.71%	35.71%	0.00%	28.57%

Table 5.3: Description Of College's Information Literacy Policy, Broken Out By FTE Enrollment

FTE Enrollment	No Specific Information Or Computer Literacy Requirement	Teaches Information/Computer Literacy Within The Framework Of The Basic English Writing Course Or Other Basic Course	Requires A One Or Two Credit Information Literacy Or Computer Literacy Course For Graduation	Requires One Or More Three Credit Information Literacy Or Computer Literacy Course For Graduation
Under 2,000 FTE Enrollment	28.57%	42.86%	0.00%	28.57%
2,000 To 10,000 FTE Enrollment	40.00%	26.67%	13.33%	20.00%
10,000+ FTE Enrollment	18.18%	63.64%	9.09%	9.09%

Table 5.4: **Description Of College's Information Literacy Policy, Broken Out By Type Of College**

Type Of College	No Specific Information Or Computer Literacy Requirement	Teaches Information/Computer Literacy Within The Framework Of The Basic English Writing Course Or Other Basic Course	Requires A One Or Two Credit Information Literacy Or Computer Literacy Course For Graduation	Requires One Or More Three Credit Information Literacy Or Computer Literacy Course For Graduation
Community College	14.29%	57.14%	14.29%	14.29%
4-Year Or MA Degree Granting Institution	32.00%	40.00%	0.00%	28.00%
PhD Granting Institution Or Research University	37.50%	37.50%	25.00%	0.00%

Chapter Six: Student Services

Table 6.1:   Percentage Of Colleges That Offer Childcare Services For Students With Children

	Yes	No
Entire Sample	46.15%	53.85%

Table 6.2:   Percentage Of Colleges That Offer Childcare Services For Students With Children, Broken Out By Public/Private Status

Public/Private	Yes	No
Public College	72.00%	28.00%
Private College	0.00%	100.00%

Table 6.3:   Percentage Of Colleges That Offer Childcare Services For Students With Children, Broken Out By FTE Enrollment

FTE Enrollment	Yes	No
Under 2,000 FTE Enrollment	21.43%	78.57%
2,000 To 10,000 FTE Enrollment	46.67%	53.33%
10,000+ FTE Enrollment	80.00%	20.00%

Table 6.4:   Percentage Of Colleges That Offer Childcare Services For Students With Children, Broken Out By Type Of College

Type Of College	Yes	No
Community College	57.14%	42.86%
4-Year Or MA Degree Granting Institution	40.00%	60.00%
PhD Granting Institution Or Research University	57.14%	42.86%

Table 6.5:   Mean, Median, Minimum And Maximum Approximate Number Of Students That Found Part Time Employment Through The College Career Services Office In The Past School Year

	Mean	Median	Minimum	Maximum
Entire Sample	21.08	12.00	0.00	55.20

Table 6.6:   Mean, Median, Minimum And Maximum Mean Approximate Number Of Students That Found Part Time Employment Through The College Career Services Office In The Past School Year, Broken Out By Public/Private Status

Public/Private	Mean	Median	Minimum	Maximum
Public College	14.60	10.00	0.00	37.00
Private College	29.50	35.00	0.00	55.20

Table 6.7:   Mean, Median, Minimum And Maximum Mean Approximate Number Of Students That Found Part Time Employment Through The College Career Services Office In The Past School Year, Broken Out By FTE Enrollment

FTE Enrollment	Mean	Median	Minimum	Maximum
Under 2,000 FTE Enrollment	23.73	20.15	0.00	55.20
2,000 To 10,000 FTE Enrollment	19.92	12.00	0.00	50.00
10,000+ FTE Enrollment	17.05	13.10	5.00	37.00

Table 6.8:   Mean, Median, Minimum And Maximum Mean Approximate Number Of Students That Found Part Time Employment Through The College Career Services Office In The Past School Year, Broken Out By Type Of College

Type Of College	Mean	Median	Minimum	Maximum
Community College	13.36	6.30	0.00	30.00
4-Year Or MA Degree Granting Institution	28.26	27.50	0.00	55.20
PhD Granting Institution Or Research University	5.60	5.20	0.00	12.00

Table 6.9:   Importance Of An Office Of Financial Aid For Success In Retention

	Very Important	Important	Somewhat Important	Infrequently Important	Not Really Important
Entire Sample	71.79%	23.08%	5.13%	0.00%	0.00%

Table 6.10: Importance Of An Office Of Financial Aid For Success In Retention, Broken Out By Public/Private Status

Public/Private	Very Important	Important	Somewhat Important	Infrequently Important	Not Really Important
Public College	72.00%	20.00%	8.00%	0.00%	0.00%
Private College	71.43%	28.57%	0.00%	0.00%	0.00%

Table 6.11: Importance Of An Office Of Financial Aid For Success In Retention, Broken Out By FTE Enrollment

FTE Enrollment	Very Important	Important	Somewhat Important	Infrequently Important	Not Really Important
Under 2,000 FTE Enrollment	78.57%	21.43%	0.00%	0.00%	0.00%
2,000 To 10,000 FTE Enrollment	66.67%	20.00%	13.33%	0.00%	0.00%
10,000+ FTE Enrollment	70.00%	30.00%	0.00%	0.00%	0.00%

Table 6.12: Importance Of An Office Of Financial Aid For Success In Retention, Broken Out By Type Of College

Type Of College	Very Important	Important	Somewhat Important	Infrequently Important	Not Really Important
Community College	71.43%	14.29%	14.29%	0.00%	0.00%
4-Year Or MA Degree Granting Institution	72.00%	24.00%	4.00%	0.00%	0.00%
PhD Granting Institution Or Research University	71.43%	28.57%	0.00%	0.00%	0.00%

Table 6.13: Importance Of Career Services For Success In Retention

	Very Important	Important	Somewhat Important	Infrequently Important	Not Really Important
Entire Sample	10.26%	41.03%	35.90%	10.26%	2.56%

Table 6.14:   Importance Of Career Services For Success In Retention, Broken Out By Public/Private Status

Public/Private	Very Important	Important	Somewhat Important	Infrequently Important	Not Really Important
Public College	12.00%	52.00%	28.00%	8.00%	0.00%
Private College	7.14%	21.43%	50.00%	14.29%	7.14%

Table 6.15:   Importance Of Career Services For Success In Retention, Broken Out By FTE Enrollment

FTE Enrollment	Very Important	Important	Somewhat Important	Infrequently Important	Not Really Important
Under 2,000 FTE Enrollment	7.14%	28.57%	50.00%	7.14%	7.14%
2,000 To 10,000 FTE Enrollment	6.67%	53.33%	26.67%	13.33%	0.00%
10,000+ FTE Enrollment	20.00%	40.00%	30.00%	10.00%	0.00%

Table 6.16:   Importance Of Career Services For Success In Retention, Broken Out By Type Of College

Type Of College	Very Important	Important	Somewhat Important	Infrequently Important	Not Really Important
Community College	0.00%	57.14%	42.86%	0.00%	0.00%
4-Year Or MA Degree Granting Institution	8.00%	40.00%	36.00%	12.00%	4.00%
PhD Granting Institution Or Research University	28.57%	28.57%	28.57%	14.29%	0.00%

Table 6.17:   Importance Of Academic Advising For Success In Retention

	Very Important	Important	Somewhat Important	Infrequently Important	Not Really Important
Entire Sample	66.67%	25.64%	7.69%	0.00%	0.00%

Table 6.18:   Importance Of Academic Advising For Success In Retention, Broken Out By Public/Private Status

Public/Private	Very Important	Important	Somewhat Important	Infrequently Important	Not Really Important
Public College	60.00%	28.00%	12.00%	0.00%	0.00%
Private College	78.57%	21.43%	0.00%	0.00%	0.00%

Table 6.19:   Importance Of Academic Advising For Success In Retention, Broken Out By FTE Enrollment

FTE Enrollment	Very Important	Important	Somewhat Important	Infrequently Important	Not Really Important
Under 2,000 FTE Enrollment	85.71%	7.14%	7.14%	0.00%	0.00%
2,000 To 10,000 FTE Enrollment	60.00%	33.33%	6.67%	0.00%	0.00%
10,000+ FTE Enrollment	50.00%	40.00%	10.00%	0.00%	0.00%

Table 6.20:   Importance Of Academic Advising For Success In Retention, Broken Out By Type Of College

Type Of College	Very Important	Important	Somewhat Important	Infrequently Important	Not Really Important
Community College	57.14%	14.29%	28.57%	0.00%	0.00%
4-Year Or MA Degree Granting Institution	68.00%	28.00%	4.00%	0.00%	0.00%
PhD Granting Institution Or Research University	71.43%	28.57%	0.00%	0.00%	0.00%

Table 6.21:   Importance Of Learning Services/Tutoring Services For Success In Retention

	Very Important	Important	Somewhat Important	Infrequently Important	Not Really Important
Entire Sample	53.85%	33.33%	12.82%	0.00%	0.00%

Table 6.22:   Importance Of Learning Services/Tutoring Services For Success In Retention, Broken Out By Public/Private Status

Public/Private	Very Important	Important	Somewhat Important	Infrequently Important	Not Really Important
Public College	52.00%	28.00%	20.00%	0.00%	0.00%
Private College	57.14%	42.86%	0.00%	0.00%	0.00%

Table 6.23:   Importance Of Learning Services/Tutoring Services For Success In Retention, Broken Out By FTE Enrollment

FTE Enrollment	Very Important	Important	Somewhat Important	Infrequently Important	Not Really Important
Under 2,000 FTE Enrollment	57.14%	35.71%	7.14%	0.00%	0.00%
2,000 To 10,000 FTE Enrollment	53.33%	26.67%	20.00%	0.00%	0.00%
10,000+ FTE Enrollment	50.00%	40.00%	10.00%	0.00%	0.00%

Table 6.24:   Importance Of Learning Services/Tutoring Services For Success In Retention, Broken Out By Type Of College

Type Of College	Very Important	Important	Somewhat Important	Infrequently Important	Not Really Important
Community College	42.86%	28.57%	28.57%	0.00%	0.00%
4-Year Or MA Degree Granting Institution	52.00%	40.00%	8.00%	0.00%	0.00%
PhD Granting Institution Or Research University	71.43%	14.29%	14.29%	0.00%	0.00%

Table 6.25:   Importance Of Peer Mentoring For Success In Retention

	Very Important	Important	Somewhat Important	Infrequently Important	Not Really Important
Entire Sample	12.82%	41.03%	33.33%	10.26%	2.56%

Table 6.26: **Importance Of Peer Mentoring For Success In Retention, Broken Out By Public/Private Status**

Public/Private	Very Important	Important	Somewhat Important	Infrequently Important	Not Really Important
Public College	12.00%	44.00%	32.00%	12.00%	0.00%
Private College	14.29%	35.71%	35.71%	7.14%	7.14%

Table 6.27: **Importance Of Peer Mentoring For Success In Retention, Broken Out By FTE Enrollment**

FTE Enrollment	Very Important	Important	Somewhat Important	Infrequently Important	Not Really Important
Under 2,000 FTE Enrollment	14.29%	28.57%	42.86%	7.14%	7.14%
2,000 To 10,000 FTE Enrollment	20.00%	26.67%	40.00%	13.33%	0.00%
10,000+ FTE Enrollment	0.00%	80.00%	10.00%	10.00%	0.00%

Table 6.28: **Importance Of Peer Mentoring For Success In Retention, Broken Out By Type Of College**

Type Of College	Very Important	Important	Somewhat Important	Infrequently Important	Not Really Important
Community College	0.00%	14.29%	71.43%	14.29%	0.00%
4-Year Or MA Degree Granting Institution	20.00%	40.00%	24.00%	12.00%	4.00%
PhD Granting Institution Or Research University	0.00%	71.43%	28.57%	0.00%	0.00%

Table 6.29: **Importance Of Childcare For Success In Retention**

	Very Important	Important	Somewhat Important	Infrequently Important	Not Really Important
Entire Sample	5.13%	15.38%	30.77%	17.95%	30.77%

Table 6.30:   Importance Of Childcare For Success In Retention, Broken Out By Public/Private Status

Public/Private	Very Important	Important	Somewhat Important	Infrequently Important	Not Really Important
Public College	8.00%	24.00%	40.00%	20.00%	8.00%
Private College	0.00%	0.00%	14.29%	14.29%	71.43%

Table 6.31:   Importance Of Childcare For Success In Retention, Broken Out By FTE Enrollment

FTE Enrollment	Very Important	Important	Somewhat Important	Infrequently Important	Not Really Important
Under 2,000 FTE Enrollment	14.29%	14.29%	7.14%	14.29%	50.00%
2,000 To 10,000 FTE Enrollment	0.00%	13.33%	46.67%	6.67%	33.33%
10,000+ FTE Enrollment	0.00%	20.00%	40.00%	40.00%	0.00%

Table 6.32:   Importance Of Childcare For Success In Retention, Broken Out By Type Of College

Type Of College	Very Important	Important	Somewhat Important	Infrequently Important	Not Really Important
Community College	14.29%	14.29%	42.86%	14.29%	14.29%
4-Year Or MA Degree Granting Institution	4.00%	16.00%	16.00%	20.00%	44.00%
PhD Granting Institution Or Research University	0.00%	14.29%	71.43%	14.29%	0.00%

Chapter Seven: Identifying The High Risk Student

Table 7.1:   Percentage Of Colleges That Say They Identify High Risk Students, And Then Intervene At Certain Thresholds Such As Number Of Classes Or Assignments Missed, Or Low Grade Point Averages

	Yes	No
Entire Sample	76.92%	23.08%

Table 7.2:   Percentage Of Colleges That Say They Identify High Risk Students, And Then Intervene At Certain Thresholds Such As Number Of Classes Or Assignments Missed, Or Low Grade Point Averages, Broken Out By Public/Private Status

Public/Private	Yes	No
Public College	72.00%	28.00%
Private College	85.71%	14.29%

Table 7.3:   Percentage Of Colleges That Say They Identify High Risk Students, And Then Intervene At Certain Thresholds Such As Number Of Classes Or Assignments Missed, Or Low Grade Point Averages, Broken Out By FTE Enrollment

FTE Enrollment	Yes	No
Under 2,000 FTE Enrollment	71.43%	28.57%
2,000 To 10,000 FTE Enrollment	80.00%	20.00%
10,000+ FTE Enrollment	80.00%	20.00%

Table 7.4:   Percentage Of Colleges That Say They Identify High Risk Students, And Then Intervene At Certain Thresholds Such As Number Of Classes Or Assignments Missed, Or Low Grade Point Averages, Broken Out By Type Of College

Type Of College	Yes	No
Community College	85.71%	14.29%
4-Year Or MA Degree Granting Institution	76.00%	24.00%
PhD Granting Institution Or Research University	71.43%	28.57%

Table 7.5: Description Of College's Efforts To Reach Out To And Help Students At High Risk For Dropping Out

	We Don't Do Enough And Are Not Really Very Good At What We Do	We Don't Do Enough And Our Present Efforts Are Passable At Best	We Make A Fairly Considerable Effort And Do As Well As Most	We Make A Great Effort But Without Great Results	We Make A Great Effort And We Have Very Good Results
Entire Sample	15.38%	33.33%	28.21%	7.69%	15.38%

Table 7.6: Description Of College's Efforts To Reach Out To And Help Students At High Risk For Dropping Out, Broken Out By Public/Private Status

Public/Private	We Don't Do Enough And Are Not Really Very Good At What We Do	We Don't Do Enough And Our Present Efforts Are Passable At Best	We Make A Fairly Considerable Effort And Do As Well As Most	We Make A Great Effort But Without Great Results	We Make A Great Effort And We Have Very Good Results
Public College	16.00%	36.00%	28.00%	4.00%	16.00%
Private College	14.29%	28.57%	28.57%	14.29%	14.29%

Table 7.7: Description Of College's Efforts To Reach Out To And Help Students At High Risk For Dropping Out, Broken Out By FTE Enrollment

FTE Enrollment	We Don't Do Enough And Are Not Really Very Good At What We Do	We Don't Do Enough And Our Present Efforts Are Passable At Best	We Make A Fairly Considerable Effort And Do As Well As Most	We Make A Great Effort But Without Great Results	We Make A Great Effort And We Have Very Good Results
Under 2,000 FTE Enrollment	7.14%	42.86%	28.57%	14.29%	7.14%
2,000 To 10,000 FTE Enrollment	26.67%	26.67%	26.67%	6.67%	13.33%
10,000+ FTE Enrollment	10.00%	30.00%	30.00%	0.00%	30.00%

Table 7.8: Description Of College's Efforts To Reach Out To And Help Students At High Risk For Dropping Out, Broken Out By Type Of College

Type Of College	We Don't Do Enough And Are Not Really Very Good At What We Do	We Don't Do Enough And Our Present Efforts Are Passable At Best	We Make A Fairly Considerable Effort And Do As Well As Most	We Make A Great Effort But Without Great Results	We Make A Great Effort And We Have Very Good Results
Community College	0.00%	42.86%	42.86%	0.00%	14.29%
4-Year Or MA Degree Granting Institution	20.00%	32.00%	28.00%	12.00%	8.00%
PhD Granting Institution Or Research University	14.29%	28.57%	14.29%	0.00%	42.86%

Chapter Eight: Tutoring

Table 8.1:   Mean, Median, Minimum And Maximum College Spending On Tutoring For All Students In The Past Year

	Mean	Median	Minimum	Maximum
Entire Sample	253,513.64	73,150.00	0.00	1,500,000.00

Table 8.2:   Mean, Median, Minimum And Maximum College Spending On Tutoring For All Students In The Past Year, Broken Out By Public/Private Status

Public/Private	Mean	Median	Minimum	Maximum
Public College	262,820.00	100,000.00	5,000.00	1,500,000.00
Private College	272,500.00	10,000.00	5,000.00	1,300,000.00

Table 8.3:   Mean, Median, Minimum And Maximum College Spending On Tutoring For All Students In The Past Year, Broken Out By FTE Enrollment

FTE Enrollment	Mean	Median	Minimum	Maximum
Under 2,000 FTE Enrollment	193,000.00	12,500.00	5,000.00	1,300,000.00
2,000 To 10,000 FTE Enrollment	116,662.50	85,650.00	10,000.00	300,000.00
10,000+ FTE Enrollment	620,000.00	150,000.00	50,000.00	1,500,000.00

Table 8.4:   Mean, Median, Minimum And Maximum College Spending On Tutoring For All Students In The Past Year, Broken Out By Type Of College

Type Of College	Mean	Median	Minimum	Maximum
Community College	62,800.00	75,000.00	5,000.00	124,000.00
4-Year Or MA Degree Granting Institution	388,561.54	100,000.00	5,000.00	1,500,000.00
PhD Granting Institution Or Research University	70,666.67	50,000.00	12,000.00	150,000.00

Table 8.5:   Mean, Median, Minimum And Maximum Projected College Spending On Tutoring For All Students In The Next Year

	Mean	Median	Minimum	Maximum
Entire Sample	279,704.76	100,000.00	0.00	1,500,000.00

Table 8.6:   Mean, Median, Minimum And Maximum Projected College Spending On Tutoring For All Students In The Next Year, Broken Out By Public/Private Status

Public/Private	Mean	Median	Minimum	Maximum
Public College	274,786.67	100,000.00	5,000.00	1,500,000.00
Private College	350,400.00	37,000.00	5,000.00	1,400,000.00

Table 8.7:   Mean, Median, Minimum And Maximum Projected College Spending On Tutoring For All Students In The Next Year, Broken Out By FTE Enrollment

FTE Enrollment	Mean	Median	Minimum	Maximum
Under 2,000 FTE Enrollment	208,875.00	26,000.00	5,000.00	1,400,000.00
2,000 To 10,000 FTE Enrollment	143,257.14	140,000.00	10,000.00	300,000.00
10,000+ FTE Enrollment	640,000.00	150,000.00	50,000.00	1,500,000.00

Table 8.8:   Mean, Median, Minimum And Maximum Projected College Spending On Tutoring For All Students In The Next Year, Broken Out By Type Of College

Type Of College	Mean	Median	Minimum	Maximum
Community College	62,800.00	75,000.00	5,000.00	124,000.00
4-Year Or MA Degree Granting Institution	445,650.00	140,400.00	5,000.00	1,500,000.00
PhD Granting Institution Or Research University	70,666.67	50,000.00	12,000.00	150,000.00

Table 8.9:   Description Of College's Attitude Towards The Impact Of A College Tutoring Program On Student Retention

	I Don't Think That Tutoring Can Have A Big Impact On Retention	We Need To Hire More Tutors, Train Them Better, Or Both	We Have A Good Tutoring Program That Has Helped Us To Maintain Or Increase Our Retention Levels	Our Tutoring Program Is Excellent And Is A Key Factor In Our Maintenance Of A Higher Than Expected Retention Level
Entire Sample	3.03%	33.33%	51.52%	12.12%

Table 8.10:   Description Of College's Attitude Towards The Impact Of A College Tutoring Program On Student Retention, Broken Out By Public/Private Status

Public/Private	I Don't Think That Tutoring Can Have A Big Impact On Retention	We Need To Hire More Tutors, Train Them Better, Or Both	We Have A Good Tutoring Program That Has Helped Us To Maintain Or Increase Our Retention Levels	Our Tutoring Program Is Excellent And Is A Key Factor In Our Maintenance Of A Higher Than Expected Retention Level
Public College	0.00%	34.78%	52.17%	13.04%
Private College	10.00%	30.00%	50.00%	10.00%

Table 8.11:   Description Of College's Attitude Towards The Impact Of A College Tutoring Program On Student Retention, Broken Out By FTE Enrollment

FTE Enrollment	I Don't Think That Tutoring Can Have A Big Impact On Retention	We Need To Hire More Tutors, Train Them Better, Or Both	We Have A Good Tutoring Program That Has Helped Us To Maintain Or Increase Our Retention Levels	Our Tutoring Program Is Excellent And Is A Key Factor In Our Maintenance Of A Higher Than Expected Retention Level
Under 2,000 FTE Enrollment	8.33%	25.00%	58.33%	8.33%
2,000 To 10,000 FTE Enrollment	0.00%	41.67%	50.00%	8.33%
10,000+ FTE Enrollment	0.00%	33.33%	44.44%	22.22%

Table 8.12:   Description Of College's Attitude Towards The Impact Of A College Tutoring Program On Student Retention, Broken Out By Type Of College

Type Of College	I Don't Think That Tutoring Can Have A Big Impact On Retention	We Need To Hire More Tutors, Train Them Better, Or Both	We Have A Good Tutoring Program That Has Helped Us To Maintain Or Increase Our Retention Levels	Our Tutoring Program Is Excellent And Is A Key Factor In Our Maintenance Of A Higher Than Expected Retention Level
Community College	0.00%	33.33%	66.67%	0.00%
4-Year Or MA Degree Granting Institution	5.00%	35.00%	50.00%	10.00%
PhD Granting Institution Or Research University	0.00%	28.57%	42.86%	28.57%

Table 8.13:   Description Of College's Tutoring Efforts

	We Don't Really Have A Formal Policy Of Any Kind	Most Tutoring Is Decentralized And Handled By Specific Academic Departments Or Administrative Agencies	Most Tutoring In Handled Through Requests To A Centralized College Agency
Entire Sample	9.09%	27.27%	63.64%

Table 8.14:   Description Of College's Tutoring Efforts, Broken Out By Public/Private Status

Public/Private	We Don't Really Have A Formal Policy Of Any Kind	Most Tutoring Is Decentralized And Handled By Specific Academic Departments Or Administrative Agencies	Most Tutoring In Handled Through Requests To A Centralized College Agency
Public College	13.04%	26.09%	60.87%
Private College	0.00%	30.00%	70.00%

Table 8.15: Description Of College's Tutoring Efforts, Broken Out By FTE Enrollment

FTE Enrollment	We Don't Really Have A Formal Policy Of Any Kind	Most Tutoring Is Decentralized And Handled By Specific Academic Departments Or Administrative Agencies	Most Tutoring In Handled Through Requests To A Centralized College Agency
Under 2,000 FTE Enrollment	0.00%	25.00%	75.00%
2,000 To 10,000 FTE Enrollment	16.67%	33.33%	50.00%
10,000+ FTE Enrollment	11.11%	22.22%	66.67%

Table 8.16: Description Of College's Tutoring Efforts, Broken Out By Type Of College

Type Of College	We Don't Really Have A Formal Policy Of Any Kind	Most Tutoring Is Decentralized And Handled By Specific Academic Departments Or Administrative Agencies	Most Tutoring In Handled Through Requests To A Centralized College Agency
Community College	0.00%	0.00%	100.00%
4-Year Or MA Degree Granting Institution	15.00%	25.00%	60.00%
PhD Granting Institution Or Research University	0.00%	57.14%	42.86%

Table 8.17: Description Of Tutors

	Other Students	Teaching Assistants Or Advanced Graduate Students Receiving Pay	Specialized Professional Tutors	Adjunct Or Full Time Faculty	All Of The Above
Entire Sample	75.76%	0.00%	6.06%	0.00%	18.18%

Table 8.18:   Description Of Tutors, Broken Out By Public/Private Status

Public/Private	Other Students	Teaching Assistants Or Advanced Graduate Students Receiving Pay	Specialized Professional Tutors	Adjunct Or Full Time Faculty	All Of The Above
Public College	69.57%	0.00%	8.70%	0.00%	21.74%
Private College	90.00%	0.00%	0.00%	0.00%	10.00%

Table 8.19:   Description Of Tutors, Broken Out By FTE Enrollment

FTE Enrollment	Other Students	Teaching Assistants Or Advanced Graduate Students Receiving Pay	Specialized Professional Tutors	Adjunct Or Full Time Faculty	All Of The Above
Under 2,000 FTE Enrollment	75.00%	0.00%	16.67%	0.00%	8.33%
2,000 To 10,000 FTE Enrollment	66.67%	0.00%	0.00%	0.00%	33.33%
10,000+ FTE Enrollment	88.89%	0.00%	0.00%	0.00%	11.11%

Table 8.20:   Description Of Tutors, Broken Out By Type Of College

Type Of College	Other Students	Teaching Assistants Or Advanced Graduate Students Receiving Pay	Specialized Professional Tutors	Adjunct Or Full Time Faculty	All Of The Above
Community College	50.00%	0.00%	16.67%	0.00%	33.33%
4-Year Or MA Degree Granting Institution	75.00%	0.00%	5.00%	0.00%	20.00%
PhD Granting Institution Or Research University	100.00%	0.00%	0.00%	0.00%	0.00%

Table 8.21:   Description Of Student Costs For Tutoring Provided By The College

	Students Do Not Pay Anything	Students Pay Some Of The Cost	Students Pay All Of The Cost
Entire Sample	81.82%	15.15%	3.03%

Table 8.22:   Description Of Student Costs For Tutoring Provided By The College, Broken Out By Public/Private Status

Public/Private	Students Do Not Pay Anything	Students Pay Some Of The Cost	Students Pay All Of The Cost
Public College	82.61%	17.39%	0.00%
Private College	80.00%	10.00%	10.00%

Table 8.23:   Description Of Student Costs For Tutoring Provided By The College, Broken Out By FTE Enrollment

FTE Enrollment	Students Do Not Pay Anything	Students Pay Some Of The Cost	Students Pay All Of The Cost
Under 2,000 FTE Enrollment	91.67%	8.33%	0.00%
2,000 To 10,000 FTE Enrollment	83.33%	8.33%	8.33%
10,000+ FTE Enrollment	66.67%	33.33%	0.00%

Table 8.24:   Description Of Student Costs For Tutoring Provided By The College, Broken Out By Type Of College

Type Of College	Students Do Not Pay Anything	Students Pay Some Of The Cost	Students Pay All Of The Cost
Community College	83.33%	16.67%	0.00%
4-Year Or MA Degree Granting Institution	85.00%	10.00%	5.00%
PhD Granting Institution Or Research University	71.43%	28.57%	0.00%

Table 8.25:   Description Of The College's Attitude Towards Tutoring Requests That Come Within The Final Three Weeks Of A The Final Regular Class In A Semester

	We Don't Really Provide Tutors	We Have A Firm Cutoff Date And Don't Take Tutoring Requests At This Time	We Have A Firm Cutoff Date Though This Is Later Than Three Weeks Before The Final Regular Class	We Don't Have A Tutoring Cutoff Date But Realistically It Is More Difficult To Meet Requests This Late In The Semester	We Don't Have A Tutoring Cutoff Date And Are Able To Serve Students Just As Well At This Time As At Other Times In The Semester
Entire Sample	6.06%	0.00%	6.06%	57.58%	30.30%

Table 8.26:   Description Of The College's Attitude Towards Tutoring Requests That Come Within The Final Three Weeks Of A The Final Regular Class In A Semester, Broken Out By Public/Private Status

Public/Private	We Don't Really Provide Tutors	We Have A Firm Cutoff Date And Don't Take Tutoring Requests At This Time	We Have A Firm Cutoff Date Though This Is Later Than Three Weeks Before The Final Regular Class	We Don't Have A Tutoring Cutoff Date But Realistically It Is More Difficult To Meet Requests This Late In The Semester	We Don't Have A Tutoring Cutoff Date And Are Able To Serve Students Just As Well At This Time As At Other Times In The Semester
Public College	8.70%	0.00%	4.35%	60.87%	26.09%
Private College	0.00%	0.00%	10.00%	50.00%	40.00%

Table 8.27: Description Of The College's Attitude Towards Tutoring Requests That Come Within The Final Three Weeks Of A The Final Regular Class In A Semester, Broken Out By FTE Enrollment

FTE Enrollment	We Don't Really Provide Tutors	We Have A Firm Cutoff Date And Don't Take Tutoring Requests At This Time	We Have A Firm Cutoff Date Though This Is Later Than Three Weeks Before The Final Regular Class	We Don't Have A Tutoring Cutoff Date But Realistically It Is More Difficult To Meet Requests This Late In The Semester	We Don't Have A Tutoring Cutoff Date And Are Able To Serve Students Just As Well At This Time As At Other Times In The Semester
Under 2,000 FTE Enrollment	0.00%	0.00%	8.33%	33.33%	58.33%
2,000 To 10,000 FTE Enrollment	8.33%	0.00%	0.00%	75.00%	16.67%
10,000+ FTE Enrollment	11.11%	0.00%	11.11%	66.67%	11.11%

Table 8.28: Description Of The College's Attitude Towards Tutoring Requests That Come Within The Final Three Weeks Of A The Final Regular Class In A Semester, Broken Out By Type Of College

Type Of College	We Don't Really Provide Tutors	We Have A Firm Cutoff Date And Don't Take Tutoring Requests At This Time	We Have A Firm Cutoff Date Though This Is Later Than Three Weeks Before The Final Regular Class	We Don't Have A Tutoring Cutoff Date But Realistically It Is More Difficult To Meet Requests This Late In The Semester	We Don't Have A Tutoring Cutoff Date And Are Able To Serve Students Just As Well At This Time As At Other Times In The Semester
Community College	0.00%	0.00%	0.00%	83.33%	16.67%
4-Year Or MA Degree Granting Institution	10.00%	0.00%	5.00%	50.00%	35.00%
PhD Granting Institution Or Research University	0.00%	0.00%	14.29%	57.14%	28.57%

Table 8.29:   Description Of The Average Per Hour Salary Of The College's Student Tutors

	They Are Unpaid	Less Than $8.00 Per Hour	$8 To $10 Per Hour	$11 To $14 Per Hour	$15 To $20 Per Hour	More Than $20 Per Hour
Entire Sample	0.00%	33.33%	46.67%	13.33%	3.33%	3.33%

Table 8.30:   Description Of The Average Per Hour Salary Of The College's Student Tutors, Broken Out By Public/Private Status

Public/Private	They Are Unpaid	Less Than $8.00 Per Hour	$8 To $10 Per Hour	$11 To $14 Per Hour	$15 To $20 Per Hour	More Than $20 Per Hour
Public College	0.00%	33.33%	47.62%	19.05%	0.00%	0.00%
Private College	0.00%	33.33%	44.44%	0.00%	11.11%	11.11%

Table 8.31:   Description Of The Average Per Hour Salary Of The College's Student Tutors, Broken Out By FTE Enrollment

FTE Enrollment	They Are Unpaid	Less Than $8.00 Per Hour	$8 To $10 Per Hour	$11 To $14 Per Hour	$15 To $20 Per Hour	More Than $20 Per Hour
Under 2,000 FTE Enrollment	0.00%	54.55%	36.36%	0.00%	0.00%	9.09%
2,000 To 10,000 FTE Enrollment	0.00%	9.09%	72.73%	9.09%	9.09%	0.00%
10,000+ FTE Enrollment	0.00%	37.50%	25.00%	37.50%	0.00%	0.00%

Table 8.32:   Description Of The Average Per Hour Salary Of The College's Student Tutors, Broken Out By Type Of College

Type Of College	They Are Unpaid	Less Than $8.00 Per Hour	$8 To $10 Per Hour	$11 To $14 Per Hour	$15 To $20 Per Hour	More Than $20 Per Hour
Community College	0.00%	40.00%	60.00%	0.00%	0.00%	0.00%
4-Year Or MA Degree Granting Institution	0.00%	27.78%	44.44%	22.22%	0.00%	5.56%
PhD Granting Institution Or Research University	0.00%	42.86%	42.86%	0.00%	14.29%	0.00%

Chapter Nine: Student Advising And Counseling

Table 9.1: Percentage Of Colleges That Have Student Advisory Centers Located In Residence Halls

	Yes	No
Entire Sample	9.38%	90.63%

Table 9.2: Percentage Of Colleges That Have Student Advisory Centers Located In Residence Halls, Broken Out By Public/Private Status

Public/Private	Yes	No
Public College	10.00%	90.00%
Private College	8.33%	91.67%

Table 9.3: Percentage Of Colleges That Have Student Advisory Centers Located In Residence Halls, Broken Out By FTE Enrollment

FTE Enrollment	Yes	No
Under 2,000 FTE Enrollment	8.33%	91.67%
2,000 To 10,000 FTE Enrollment	7.69%	92.31%
10,000+ FTE Enrollment	14.29%	85.71%

Table 9.4: Percentage Of Colleges That Have Student Advisory Centers Located In Residence Halls, Broken Out By Type Of College

	Yes	No
Community College	0.00%	100.00%
4-Year Or MA Degree Granting Institution	0.00%	100.00%
PhD Granting Institution Or Research University	50.00%	50.00%

Table 9.5: Percentage Of Colleges That Have Ever Hired A Consultant To Review Or Advise On The College's Academic Advising Services

	Yes	No
Entire Sample	21.21%	78.79%

Table 9.6: Percentage Of Colleges That Have Ever Hired A Consultant To Review Or Advise On The College's Academic Advising Services, Broken Out By Public/Private Status

Public/Private	Yes	No
Public College	19.05%	80.95%
Private College	25.00%	75.00%

Table 9.7: Percentage Of Colleges That Have Ever Hired A Consultant To Review Or Advise On The College's Academic Advising Services, Broken Out By FTE Enrollment

FTE Enrollment	Yes	No
Under 2,000 FTE Enrollment	8.33%	91.67%
2,000 To 10,000 FTE Enrollment	15.38%	84.62%
10,000+ FTE Enrollment	50.00%	50.00%

Table 9.8: Percentage Of Colleges That Have Ever Hired A Consultant To Review Or Advise On The College's Academic Advising Services, Broken Out By Type Of College

Type Of College	Yes	No
Community College	0.00%	100.00%
4-Year Or MA Degree Granting Institution	27.27%	72.73%
PhD Granting Institution Or Research University	16.67%	83.33%

Table 9.9: Percentage Of Colleges That Have Ever Hired A Consultant To Review The College's Academic Advising Services
Table 9.10:

	Yes	No
Entire Sample	21.88%	78.13%

Table 9.11: Percentage Of Colleges That Have Ever Hired A Consultant To Review The College's Academic Advising Services, Broken Out By Public/Private Status

Public/Private	Yes	No
Public College	19.05%	80.95%
Private College	27.27%	72.73%

Table 9.12:   Percentage Of Colleges That Have Ever Hired A Consultant To Review The College's Academic Advising Services, Broken Out By FTE Enrollment

FTE Enrollment	Yes	No
Under 2,000 FTE Enrollment	9.09%	90.91%
2,000 To 10,000 FTE Enrollment	15.38%	84.62%
10,000+ FTE Enrollment	50.00%	50.00%

Table 9.13:   Percentage Of Colleges That Have Ever Hired A Consultant To Review The College's Academic Advising Services, Broken Out By Type Of College

Type Of College	Yes	No
Community College	0.00%	100.00%
4-Year Or MA Degree Granting Institution	28.57%	71.43%
PhD Granting Institution Or Research University	16.67%	83.33%

Table 9.14:   Mean, Median, Minimum And Maximum Total Annual Budget, Including Spending For Salaries, Of The College's Academic Advising Unit

	Mean	Median	Minimum	Maximum
Entire Sample	695,625.00	380,000.00	0.00	5,000,000.00

Table 9.15:   Mean, Median, Minimum And Maximum Total Annual Budget, Including Spending For Salaries, Of The College's Academic Advising Unit, Broken Out By Public/Private Status

Public/Private	Mean	Median	Minimum	Maximum
Public College	966,363.64	500,000.00	70,000.00	5,000,000.00
Private College	250,000.00	250,000.00	0.00	500,000.00

Table 9.16:   Mean, Median, Minimum And Maximum Total Annual Budget, Including Spending For Salaries, Of The College's Academic Advising Unit, Broken Out By FTE Enrollment

FTE Enrollment	Mean	Median	Minimum	Maximum
Under 2,000 FTE Enrollment	450,000.00	450,000.00	70,000.00	830,000.00
2,000 To 10,000 FTE Enrollment	353,750.00	380,000.00	0.00	750,000.00
10,000+ FTE Enrollment	2,466,666.67	1,200,000.00	1,200,000.00	5,000,000.00

Table 9.17:   Mean, Median, Minimum And Maximum Total Annual Budget, Including Spending For Salaries, Of The College's Academic Advising Unit, Broken Out By Type Of College

Type Of College	Mean	Median	Minimum	Maximum
Community College	466,666.67	500,000.00	70,000.00	830,000.00
4-Year Or MA Degree Granting Institution	1,062,222.22	500,000.00	0.00	5,000,000.00
PhD Granting Institution Or Research University	170,000.00	170,000.00	170,000.00	170,000.00

Table 9.18:   Mean, Median, Minimum And Maximum Number Of Full Time Equivalent Positions Allocated To The Department Of Academic Advising Or Its Equivalent

	Mean	Median	Minimum	Maximum
Entire Sample	14.57	9.00	0.00	116.00

Table 9.19:   Mean, Median, Minimum And Maximum Number Of Full Time Equivalent Positions Allocated To The Department Of Academic Advising Or Its Equivalent, Broken Out By Public/Private Status

Public/Private	Mean	Median	Minimum	Maximum
Public College	18.88	10.00	2.00	116.00
Private College	3.08	2.25	0.00	10.00

Table 9.20:   Mean, Median, Minimum And Maximum Number Of Full Time Equivalent Positions Allocated To The Department Of Academic Advising Or Its Equivalent, Broken Out By FTE Enrollment

FTE Enrollment	Mean	Median	Minimum	Maximum
Under 2,000 FTE Enrollment	2.33	2.00	0.00	5.00
2,000 To 10,000 FTE Enrollment	7.45	9.00	0.00	12.00
10,000+ FTE Enrollment	38.67	19.00	15.00	116.00

Table 9.21: **Mean, Median, Minimum And Maximum Number Of Full Time Equivalent Positions Allocated To The Department Of Academic Advising Or Its Equivalent, Broken Out By Type Of College**

Type Of College	Mean	Median	Minimum	Maximum
Community College	6.25	6.50	2.00	10.00
4-Year Or MA Degree Granting Institution	15.67	10.00	0.00	116.00
PhD Granting Institution Or Research University	20.17	12.00	3.50	45.00

Chapter Ten: Financial Aid & Student Employment

Table 10.1:   Description Of The Growth Of The College's Financial Aid Over The Past Two Years

	It Has Become Much Less Generous	It Has Become Somewhat Less Generous	It Has Remained About The Same In Real Terms	It Has Become Somewhat More Generous	It Has Become Much More Generous
Entire Sample	6.45%	12.90%	54.84%	25.81%	0.00%

Table 10.2:   Description Of The Growth Of The College's Financial Aid Over The Past Two Years, Broken Out By Public/Private Status

Public/Private	It Has Become Much Less Generous	It Has Become Somewhat Less Generous	It Has Remained About The Same In Real Terms	It Has Become Somewhat More Generous	It Has Become Much More Generous
Public College	4.76%	14.29%	61.90%	19.05%	0.00%
Private College	10.00%	10.00%	40.00%	40.00%	0.00%

Table 10.3:   Description Of The Growth Of The College's Financial Aid Over The Past Two Years, Broken Out By FTE Enrollment

FTE Enrollment	It Has Become Much Less Generous	It Has Become Somewhat Less Generous	It Has Remained About The Same In Real Terms	It Has Become Somewhat More Generous	It Has Become Much More Generous
Under 2,000 FTE Enrollment	0.00%	0.00%	54.55%	45.45%	0.00%
2,000 To 10,000 FTE Enrollment	16.67%	33.33%	41.67%	8.33%	0.00%
10,000+ FTE Enrollment	0.00%	0.00%	75.00%	25.00%	0.00%

Table 10.4:   Description Of The Growth Of The College's Financial Aid Over The Past Two Years, Broken Out By Type Of College

Type Of College	It Has Become Much Less Generous	It Has Become Somewhat Less Generous	It Has Remained About The Same In Real Terms	It Has Become Somewhat More Generous	It Has Become Much More Generous
Community College	0.00%	0.00%	60.00%	40.00%	0.00%
4-Year Or MA Degree Granting Institution	5.00%	15.00%	50.00%	30.00%	0.00%
PhD Granting Institution Or Research University	16.67%	16.67%	66.67%	0.00%	0.00%

Table 10.5:   Description Of Tuition Levels And The Financial Situation Of The Student Body

	It Has Become More And More Difficult For Our Students To Pay For College	The Overall Financial Burden On Our Students Has Not Changed Much In Recent Years	Our Aid Programs And A Strong Economy Have Actually Reduced The Financial Burden On Our Students In Recent Years
Entire Sample	61.29%	35.48%	3.23%

Table 10.6:   Description Of Tuition Levels And The Financial Situation Of The Student Body, Broken Out By Public/Private Status

Public/Private	It Has Become More And More Difficult For Our Students To Pay For College	The Overall Financial Burden On Our Students Has Not Changed Much In Recent Years	Our Aid Programs And A Strong Economy Have Actually Reduced The Financial Burden On Our Students In Recent Years
Public College	57.14%	38.10%	4.76%
Private College	70.00%	30.00%	0.00%

Table 10.7:   Description Of Tuition Levels And The Financial Situation Of The Student Body, Broken Out By FTE Enrollment

FTE Enrollment	It Has Become More And More Difficult For Our Students To Pay For College	The Overall Financial Burden On Our Students Has Not Changed Much In Recent Years	Our Aid Programs And A Strong Economy Have Actually Reduced The Financial Burden On Our Students In Recent Years
Under 2,000 FTE Enrollment	72.73%	27.27%	0.00%
2,000 To 10,000 FTE Enrollment	50.00%	41.67%	8.33%
10,000+ FTE Enrollment	62.50%	37.50%	0.00%

Table 10.8:   Description Of Tuition Levels And The Financial Situation Of The Student Body, Broken Out By Type Of College

Type Of College	It Has Become More And More Difficult For Our Students To Pay For College	The Overall Financial Burden On Our Students Has Not Changed Much In Recent Years	Our Aid Programs And A Strong Economy Have Actually Reduced The Financial Burden On Our Students In Recent Years
Community College	20.00%	60.00%	20.00%
4-Year Or MA Degree Granting Institution	75.00%	25.00%	0.00%
PhD Granting Institution Or Research University	50.00%	50.00%	0.00%

Table 10.9:   Description Of Necessary Changes To Tuition To Take Over The Next Few Years In Order To Retain Or Enhance The Quality Of Students That Are Attracted To The Institution, And To Maintain Or Increase Enrollment

	Lower Tuition, Increase Financial Aid Or Both	Not Make Any Serious Changes In This Way	We Can Increase Tuition And Still Attract The Same Quality And Number Of Students
Entire Sample	35.48%	38.71%	25.81%

Table 10.10: Description Of Necessary Changes To Tuition To Take Over The Next Few Years In Order To Retain Or Enhance The Quality Of Students That Are Attracted To The Institution, And To Maintain Or Increase Enrollment, Broken Out By Public/Private Status

Public/Private	Lower Tuition, Increase Financial Aid Or Both	Not Make Any Serious Changes In This Way	We Can Increase Tuition And Still Attract The Same Quality And Number Of Students
Public College	28.57%	47.62%	23.81%
Private College	50.00%	20.00%	30.00%

Table 10.11: Description Of Necessary Changes To Tuition To Take Over The Next Few Years In Order To Retain Or Enhance The Quality Of Students That Are Attracted To The Institution, And To Maintain Or Increase Enrollment, Broken Out By FTE Enrollment

FTE Enrollment	Lower Tuition, Increase Financial Aid Or Both	Not Make Any Serious Changes In This Way	We Can Increase Tuition And Still Attract The Same Quality And Number Of Students
Under 2,000 FTE Enrollment	63.64%	27.27%	9.09%
2,000 To 10,000 FTE Enrollment	25.00%	41.67%	33.33%
10,000+ FTE Enrollment	12.50%	50.00%	37.50%

Table 10.12: Description Of Necessary Changes To Tuition To Take Over The Next Few Years In Order To Retain Or Enhance The Quality Of Students That Are Attracted To The Institution, And To Maintain Or Increase Enrollment, Broken Out By Type Of College

Type Of College	Lower Tuition, Increase Financial Aid Or Both	Not Make Any Serious Changes In This Way	We Can Increase Tuition And Still Attract The Same Quality And Number Of Students
Community College	0.00%	80.00%	20.00%
4-Year Or MA Degree Granting Institution	50.00%	30.00%	20.00%
PhD Granting Institution Or Research University	16.67%	33.33%	50.00%

Chapter Eleven: Training A Retention-Minded Staff

Table 11.1: Description Of Institution's Attitude Towards Encouraging Student-Instructor Interaction Outside Of The Classroom

	Don't Really Have A Policy On This Issue	Encourage This Contact In A Casual Way	Encourage Faculty To Reach Out To Students In Extra-Curricular Work, Extended Office Hours, Attendance At Campus Events And Other Forms Of Participation With Students
Entire Sample	22.58%	22.58%	54.84%

Table 11.2: Description Of Institution's Attitude Towards Encouraging Student-Instructor Interaction Outside Of The Classroom, Broken Out By Public/Private Status

Public/Private	Don't Really Have A Policy On This Issue	Encourage This Contact In A Casual Way	Encourage Faculty To Reach Out To Students In Extra-Curricular Work, Extended Office Hours, Attendance At Campus Events And Other Forms Of Participation With Students
Public College	23.81%	23.81%	52.38%
Private College	20.00%	20.00%	60.00%

Table 11.3:   Description Of Institution's Attitude Towards Encouraging Student-Instructor Interaction Outside Of The Classroom, Broken Out By FTE Enrollment

FTE Enrollment	Don't Really Have A Policy On This Issue	Encourage This Contact In A Casual Way	Encourage Faculty To Reach Out To Students In Extra-Curricular Work, Extended Office Hours, Attendance At Campus Events And Other Forms Of Participation With Students
Under 2,000 FTE Enrollment	27.27%	18.18%	54.55%
2,000 To 10,000 FTE Enrollment	8.33%	25.00%	66.67%
10,000+ FTE Enrollment	37.50%	25.00%	37.50%

Table 11.4:   Description Of Institution's Attitude Towards Encouraging Student-Instructor Interaction Outside Of The Classroom, Broken Out By Type Of College

Type Of College			
Community College	40.00%	0.00%	60.00%
4-Year Or MA Degree Granting Institution	20.00%	20.00%	60.00%
PhD Granting Institution Or Research University	16.67%	50.00%	33.33%

Survey of Student Retention Policies in Higher Education

We asked the sample if their college has had some success in training the college staff and instructors in retention issues, and to briefly explain what they have done.

1. Noel levitz retention analysis, presentations to departments, creating an assessment and retention analysis council, a new president with a focus on student success.
2. Presentations, participation in meetings, personal contact.
3. The connection between faculty, support staff and students is strong. Staff coined their motto as: "I am committed to your success." We have a college-wide staff development day with one thread being retention. The opening speaker usually has a message about how retention can be increased. A number of projects have been implemented for staff to research or implement pilot projects. Significant number of staff assist student gain provincial and federal grants for study. These staff are further researching how the grant structures can further assist students.
4. Implemented a new probation policy and intervention program that intends to better connect students with their academic adviser, resulting in a higher # of referrals to other campus services.
5. Our enrollment management team has distributed a list of activities that faculty can do to enhance retention and graduation rates of students. We also have workshops each semester that focus on recruitment, retention, and graduation rates.
6. Retreat, in-house marketing publications.
7. Two years ago we hired a retention coordinator with full-time responsibility for retention challenges. Extensive tracking by institutional research with findings passed on to faculty & staff
8. Faculty-staff development holds regular workshops for faculty & staff on effective teaching and informational sessions with demographics/characteristics of students, with suggestions on working and communicating with them.
9. Over 95% of entering students take first-year seminars, and the FYS faculty are the primary advisors until students declare a major. We are experimenting with student peer writing tutors in about 50% of seminars. We organize peer-assisted learning groups for several difficult courses.
10. Our Title III grant included a strong faculty development component. Student retention was included throughout the programs as opposed to presenting one workshop that covered retention strategies.
11. Presentations and surveys/reports by enrollment services, institutional research and faculty have been conducted or distributed to the college cabinet, faculty and administrative offices.

Chapter Twelve: Strategies For Special Populations

Table 12.1:   Mean, Median, Minimum And Maximum Approximate Percentage Of Students In The Sample Colleges That Were Born Abroad

	Mean	Median	Minimum	Maximum
Entire Sample	8.66	4.50	0.00	35.00

Table 12.2:   Mean, Median, Minimum And Maximum Approximate Percentage Of Students In The Sample Colleges That Were Born Abroad, Broken Out By Public/Private Status

Public/Private	Mean	Median	Minimum	Maximum
Public College	7.91	4.00	0.00	35.00
Private College	10.80	8.00	0.00	35.00

Table 12.3:   Mean, Median, Minimum And Maximum Approximate Percentage Of Students In The Sample Colleges That Were Born Abroad, Broken Out By FTE Enrollment

FTE Enrollment	Mean	Median	Minimum	Maximum
Under 2,000 FTE Enrollment	6.25	1.50	0.00	23.00
2,000 To 10,000 FTE Enrollment	9.73	5.00	1.00	35.00
10,000+ FTE Enrollment	12.17	12.50	1.50	22.50

Table 12.4:   Mean, Median, Minimum And Maximum Approximate Percentage Of Students In The Sample Colleges That Were Born Abroad, Broken Out By Type Of College

Type Of College	Mean	Median	Minimum	Maximum
Community College	7.50	1.00	0.00	35.00
4-Year Or MA Degree Granting Institution	8.86	8.00	0.00	23.00
PhD Granting Institution Or Research University	11.38	4.50	1.50	35.00

Table 12.5:   Mean, Median, Minimum And Maximum Approximate Percentage Of The Students In The Sample Colleges That Started As Freshmen Or Transferees In The Past Year That Need Special Help In Reading, Writing Or Pronouncing The English Language In Order To Have A Good Chance At Being Effective College Students

	Mean	Median	Minimum	Maximum
Entire Sample	27.50	15.00	0.00	85.00

Table 12.6:   Mean, Median, Minimum And Maximum Approximate Percentage Of The Students In The Sample Colleges That Started As Freshmen Or Transferees In The Past Year That Need Special Help In Reading, Writing Or Pronouncing The English Language In Order To Have A Good Chance At Being Effective College Students, Broken Out By Public/Private Status

Public/Private	Mean	Median	Minimum	Maximum
Public College	35.81	42.50	0.50	85.00
Private College	12.56	7.50	0.00	45.00

Table 12.7:   Mean, Median, Minimum And Maximum Approximate Percentage Of The Students In The Sample Colleges That Started As Freshmen Or Transferees In The Past Year That Need Special Help In Reading, Writing Or Pronouncing The English Language In Order To Have A Good Chance At Being Effective College Students, Broken Out By FTE Enrollment

FTE Enrollment	Mean	Median	Minimum	Maximum
Under 2,000 FTE Enrollment	23.11	10.00	0.00	85.00
2,000 To 10,000 FTE Enrollment	26.71	15.00	0.50	70.00
10,000+ FTE Enrollment	36.42	47.50	0.50	58.00

Survey of Student Retention Policies in Higher Education

Table 12.8: Mean, Median, Minimum And Maximum Approximate Percentage Of The Students In The Sample Colleges That Started As Freshmen Or Transferees In The Past Year That Need Special Help In Reading, Writing Or Pronouncing The English Language In Order To Have A Good Chance At Being Effective College Students, Broken Out By Type Of College

Type Of College	Mean	Median	Minimum	Maximum
Community College	17.20	15.00	1.00	40.00
4-Year Or MA Degree Granting Institution	30.43	27.50	0.00	85.00
PhD Granting Institution Or Research University	25.17	15.00	0.50	60.00

Table 12.9: Percentage Of Colleges That Offer English As A Second Language Courses

	Yes	No
Entire Sample	58.06%	41.94%

Table 12.10: Percentage Of Colleges That Offer English As A Second Language Courses, Broken Out By Public/Private Status

Public/Private	Yes	No
Public College	66.67%	33.33%
Private College	40.00%	60.00%

Table 12.11: Percentage Of Colleges That Offer English As A Second Language Courses, Broken Out By FTE Enrollment

FTE Enrollment	Yes	No
Under 2,000 FTE Enrollment	36.36%	63.64%
2,000 To 10,000 FTE Enrollment	58.33%	41.67%
10,000+ FTE Enrollment	87.50%	12.50%

Table 12.12: Percentage Of Colleges That Offer English As A Second Language Courses, Broken Out By Type Of College

Type Of College	Yes	No
Community College	60.00%	40.00%
4-Year Or MA Degree Granting Institution	55.00%	45.00%
PhD Granting Institution Or Research University	66.67%	33.33%

Survey of Student Retention Policies in Higher Education

We asked the sample to describe the best tools, policies or methods that they have found to ease the experience of immigrant or foreign students and increase the college's retention of this population:

1. No real focus.
2. Uncertain.
3. Unfortunately, most of our time and staffing is spent on compliance rather than providing services. We have a dinner for them at the beginning of the semester. We used to do a lot more but don't have funds or staff. Lacking an ESL program, I worry about not being able to provide enough help for students.
4. Flexibility and listening to student needs.
5. Extensive orientation program, good student centered ESL instructors, one-on-one language tutorial.
6. Some developmental classes specifically for non-native speakers of English.
7. Formation of an international student office.
8. Providing special peer and faculty assistance and tutorials.
9. Being a part of an athletic team.
10. Advising.
11. Improved the international student organization; improved communication between the office of admission and student affairs regarding this population; developing a connecting cultures program.
12. Good orientation, lots of staff attention.
13. Most adjustments have been cultural rather than language-based, so we have informational sessions on living in the U.S. that includes information on opening a bank account, using school services (health clinic, etc).
14. A dean of students is largely dedicated to working with foreign students. We conduct a special pre-orientation for them. Dorms are open during vacation, and we try to connect students with local families for holiday meals.
15. Having a specific advisor/counselor who works exclusively for those students.
16. Specific office with staff to assist students with the transition and to educate university staff.
17. Special inter-nation orientation and peer leaders; special composition class (year long); ESL writing lab; we offer note takers for new ESL learners in the classes they have difficulty in following lectures; special workshops offered on pertinent topics (i.e., plagiarism) held throughout the year.
18. Dedicated adviser.

Chapter Thirteen: Retention Rate Trends

Table 13.1: Description Of The College's Retention Rate For First Year Students Entering Their Second Year

	It Has Remained About The Same For The Past Two Years	It Has Increased In The Past Two Years	It Has Decreased In The Past Two Years
Entire Sample	58.06%	22.58%	19.35%

Table 13.2: Description Of The College's Retention Rate For First Year Students Entering Their Second Year, Broken Out By Public/Private Status

Public/Private	It Has Remained About The Same For The Past Two Years	It Has Increased In The Past Two Years	It Has Decreased In The Past Two Years
Public College	61.90%	28.57%	9.52%
Private College	50.00%	10.00%	40.00%

Table 13.3: Description Of The College's Retention Rate For First Year Students Entering Their Second Year, Broken Out By FTE Enrollment

FTE Enrollment	It Has Remained About The Same For The Past Two Years	It Has Increased In The Past Two Years	It Has Decreased In The Past Two Years
Under 2,000 FTE Enrollment	63.64%	9.09%	27.27%
2,000 To 10,000 FTE Enrollment	50.00%	25.00%	25.00%
10,000+ FTE Enrollment	62.50%	37.50%	0.00%

Table 13.4: Description Of The College's Retention Rate For First Year Students Entering Their Second Year, Broken Out By Type Of College

Type Of College	It Has Remained About The Same For The Past Two Years	It Has Increased In The Past Two Years	It Has Decreased In The Past Two Years
Community College	80.00%	20.00%	0.00%
4-Year Or MA Degree Granting Institution	55.00%	20.00%	25.00%
PhD Granting Institution Or Research University	50.00%	33.33%	16.67%

Table 13.5:   Mean, Median, Minimum And Maximum Percentage Of Students Who Drop Out Who do so Primarily For Economic Reasons

	Mean	Median	Minimum	Maximum
Entire Sample	25.74	16.50	0.00	65.00

Table 13.6:   Mean, Median, Minimum And Maximum Percentage Of Students Who Drop Out Who do so Primarily For Economic Reasons, Broken Out By Public/Private Status

Public/Private	Mean	Median	Minimum	Maximum
Public College	30.94	30.00	2.00	65.00
Private College	17.43	14.65	0.00	50.00

Table 13.7:   Mean, Median, Minimum And Maximum Percentage Of Students Who Drop Out Who do so Primarily For Economic Reasons, Broken Out By FTE Enrollment

FTE Enrollment	Mean	Median	Minimum	Maximum
Under 2,000 FTE Enrollment	29.48	30.00	5.00	50.00
2,000 To 10,000 FTE Enrollment	20.73	10.00	0.00	60.00
10,000+ FTE Enrollment	29.25	25.00	2.00	65.00

Table 13.8:   Mean, Median, Minimum And Maximum Percentage Of Students Who Drop Out Who do so Primarily For Economic Reasons, Broken Out By Type Of College

Type Of College	Mean	Median	Minimum	Maximum
Community College	31.50	40.00	7.50	50.00
4-Year Or MA Degree Granting Institution	25.93	16.50	2.00	65.00
PhD Granting Institution Or Research University	15.00	5.00	0.00	40.00

Table 13.9:   Sample Colleges' Predicted Trend In Retention Rates Over The Next Few Years

	Our Retention Rates Will Probably Decline	Our Retention Rates Will Probably Stay About The Same	Our Retention Rates Will Increase
Entire Sample	6.45%	35.48%	58.06%

Table 13.10:   Sample Colleges' Predicted Trend In Retention Rates Over The Next Few Years, Broken Out By Public/Private Status

Public/Private	Our Retention Rates Will Probably Decline	Our Retention Rates Will Probably Stay About The Same	Our Retention Rates Will Increase
Public College	4.76%	42.86%	52.38%
Private College	10.00%	20.00%	70.00%

Table 13.11:   Sample Colleges' Predicted Trend In Retention Rates Over The Next Few Years, Broken Out By FTE Enrollment

FTE Enrollment	Our Retention Rates Will Probably Decline	Our Retention Rates Will Probably Stay About The Same	Our Retention Rates Will Increase
Under 2,000 FTE Enrollment	0.00%	54.55%	45.45%
2,000 To 10,000 FTE Enrollment	16.67%	8.33%	75.00%
10,000+ FTE Enrollment	0.00%	50.00%	50.00%

Table 13.12:   Sample Colleges' Predicted Trend In Retention Rates Over The Next Few Years, Broken Out By Type Of College

Type Of College	Our Retention Rates Will Probably Decline	Our Retention Rates Will Probably Stay About The Same	Our Retention Rates Will Increase
Community College	0.00%	60.00%	40.00%
4-Year Or MA Degree Granting Institution	0.00%	35.00%	65.00%
PhD Granting Institution Or Research University	33.33%	16.67%	50.00%

Chapter Fourteen: Learning Communities

Table 14.1:   Percentage Of Colleges That Have Ever Developed A "Learning Community", Or A Group Of Students Who Take More Than One Class Together, And Who Form A Faculty-Assisted Academic Support Group For One Another

	Yes, We Use This Tactic Often	Yes, But Not With Great Success	No
Entire Sample	40.00%	36.67%	23.33%

Table 14.2:   Percentage Of Colleges That Have Ever Developed A "Learning Community", Or A Group Of Students Who Take More Than One Class Together, And Who Form A Faculty-Assisted Academic Support Group For One Another, Broken Out By Public/Private Status

Public/Private	Yes, We Use This Tactic Often	Yes, But Not With Great Success	No
Public College	40.00%	40.00%	20.00%
Private College	40.00%	30.00%	30.00%

Table 14.3:   Percentage Of Colleges That Have Ever Developed A "Learning Community", Or A Group Of Students Who Take More Than One Class Together, And Who Form A Faculty-Assisted Academic Support Group For One Another, Broken Out By FTE Enrollment

FTE Enrollment	Yes, We Use This Tactic Often	Yes, But Not With Great Success	No
Under 2,000 FTE Enrollment	27.27%	36.36%	36.36%
2,000 To 10,000 FTE Enrollment	27.27%	54.55%	18.18%
10,000+ FTE Enrollment	75.00%	12.50%	12.50%

Table 14.4:   Percentage Of Colleges That Have Ever Developed A "Learning Community", Or A Group Of Students Who Take More Than One Class Together, And Who Form A Faculty-Assisted Academic Support Group For One Another, Broken Out By Type Of College

Type Of College	Yes, We Use This Tactic Often	Yes, But Not With Great Success	No
Community College	25.00%	75.00%	0.00%
4-Year Or MA Degree Granting Institution	35.00%	35.00%	30.00%
PhD Granting Institution Or Research University	66.67%	16.67%	16.67%

Other Reports from Primary Research Group, Inc.

THE SURVEY OF LIBRARY DATABASE LICENSING PRACTICES
ISBN: 1-57440-093-2   Price: $80.00   Publication Date: December 2007
The study presents data from 90 libraries – corporate, legal, college, public, state, and nonprofit libraries – about their database licensing practices. More than half of the participating libraries are from the U.S., and the rest are from Canada, Australia, the U.K., and other countries. Data are broken out by type and size of library, as well as for overall level of database expenditure. The 100+-page study, with more than 400 tables and charts, presents benchmarking data enabling librarians to compare their library's practices to peers in many areas related to licensing. Metrics provided include: percentage of licenses from consortiums, spending on consortium dues, time spent seeking new consortium partners, number of consortium memberships maintained; growth rate in the percentage of licenses obtained through consortiums; expectation for consortium purchases in the future; number of licenses, growth rate in the number of licenses, spending on licenses for directories, electronic journals, e-books, and magazine/newspaper databases; future spending plans on all of the above; price inflation experienced for electronic resources in business, medical, humanities, financial, market research, social sciences and many other information categories; price inflation for e-books, electronic directories, journals and newspaper/magazine databases; percentage of licenses that require passwords; percentage of licenses that have simultaneous access restrictions; spending on legal services related to licenses, and much more.

THE INTERNATIONAL SURVEY OF INSTITUTIONAL DIGITAL REPOSITORIES
ISBN: 1-57440-090-8   Price: $89.50   Publication Date: November 2007

The study presents data from 56 institutional digital repositories from 11 countries, including the U.S., Canada, Australia, Germany, South Africa, India, Turkey and other countries. The 121-page study presents more than 300 tables of data and commentary and is based on data from higher education libraries and other institutions involved in institutional digital repository development. In more than 300 tables and associated commentary, the report describes norms and benchmarks for budgets, software use, manpower needs and deployment, financing, usage, marketing and other facets of the management of international digital repositories. The report helps to answer questions such as: who contributes to the repositories and on what terms? Who uses the repositories? What do they contain and how fast are they growing in terms of content and end use? What measures have repositories used to gain faculty and other researcher participation? How successful have these methods been? How has the repository been marketed and cataloged? What has been the financial impact? Data is broken out by size and type of institution for easier benchmarking.

ACADEMIC LIBRARY WEBSITE BENCHMARKS
ISBN: 1-57440-094-0   Price: $85.00   Publication Date: January 2008

This report is based on data from more than 80 academic libraries in the U.S. and Canada. The 125+-page study presents detailed data on the composition of the academic library Web staff, relations with the college and library information technology departments, use of consultants and freelancers, budgets, future plans, Website marketing methods, Website revision plans, usage statistics, use of software, development of federated search and online forms and much more. Data is broken out by enrollment size, public and private status, Carnegie Class, as well as for libraries with or without their own Web staff.

PREVAILING & BEST PRACTICES IN ELECTRONIC AND PRINT SERIALS MANAGEMENT
ISBN: 1- 57440-076-2   Price: $80.00   Publication Date: November 2005

This report looks closely at the electronic and print serials procurement and management practices of 11 libraries, including: the University of Ohio, Villanova University, the Colorado School of Mines, Carleton College, Northwestern University, Baylor University, Princeton University, the University of Pennsylvania, the University of San Francisco, Embry-Riddle Aeronautical University and the University of Nebraska Medical Center. The report looks at both electronic and print serials and includes discussions of the following issues: selection and management of serials agents, including the negotiation of payment; allocating the serials budget by department; resolving access issues with publishers; use of consortiums in journal licensing; invoice reconciliation and payment; periodicals binding, claims, check-in and management; serials department staff size and range of responsibilities; serials management software; use of open access archives and university depositories; policies on gift subscriptions, free trials and academic exchanges of publications; use of electronic serials/catalog linking technology; acquisition of usage statistics; cooperative arrangements with other local libraries and other issues in serials management.

CREATING THE DIGITAL ART LIBRARY
Price: $80.00   Publication Date: October 2005

This special report looks at the efforts of 10 leading art libraries and image collections to digitize their holdings. The study reports on the efforts of the National Gallery of Canada, Cornell University's Knight Resource Center, the University of North Carolina, Chapel Hill; the Smithsonian Institution Libraries, the Illinois Institute of Technology, The National Archives and Records Administration, McGill University, Ohio State University, the Cleveland Museum of Art, and the joint effort of Harvard, Princeton, the University of California, San Diego, the University of Minnesota and others to develop a union catalog for cultural objects.

Among the issues covered: cost of outsourcing, cost of in-house conversions, the future of 35mm slides and related equipment, use of ARTstor and other commercial services, ease of interlibrary loan in images and the creation of a union catalog, prioritizing holdings for digitization, relationship of art libraries to departmental image collections, marketing image collections, range of end users of image collections, determining levels of access to the collection, digitization and distribution of backup materials on artists lives and times, equipment selection, copyright, and other issues in the creation and maintenance of digital art libraries.

TRENDS IN MANAGEMENT OF LIBRARY SPECIAL COLLECTIONS IN FILM AND PHOTOGRAPHY
ISBN: 1-57440-001-01   Price: $80.00:   Publication Date: October 2005
This special report looks at the management and development of America's thriving special collections in film and photography. The report profiles the following collections: the University of Louisville, the Photographic Archives, the University of Utah's Multimedia Collection, The American Institute of Physics' Emilio Segre Visual Archives, the Newsfilm Library at the University of South Carolina, The University of California, Berkeley Pacific Film Archive; the UCLA Film and Television Archive, the Vanderbilt University Television News Archive, the National Archives and Records Administration's Special Media Preservation Laboratory; the University of Washington's Digital Initiatives.

The report covers digitization of photographs and film, special collection marketing, collection procurement, funding and financing, approaches for optimizing both sales revenues and educational uses, development of Web-based sale and distribution systems for photography and film, systems to assure copyright compliance, the development of online searchable databases, and many other aspects of film and photography special collections management.

THE MARKETING OF HISTORIC SITES, MUSEUMS, EXHIBITS AND ARCHIVES
ISBN: 1-57440-074-6   Price: $95.00   Publication Date: June 2005
This report looks closely at how history is presented and marketed by organizations such as history museums, libraries, historical societies, and historic sites and monuments. The report profiles the efforts of the Vermont Historical Society, Hook's Historic Drug Store and Pharmacy, the Thomas Jefferson Foundation/Monticello, the Musee Conti Wax Museum of New Orleans, the Bostonian Society, the Dittrick Medical History Center, the Band Museum, the Belmont Mansion, the Kansas State Historical Society, the Computer History Museum, the Atari Virtual Museum, the Museum of American Financial History, the Atlanta History Center and the public libraries of Denver and Evansville. The study's revealing profiles, based on extensive interviews with executive directors and marketing managers of the institutions cited, provide a deeply detailed look at how history museums, sites, societies and monuments are marketing themselves.

LICENSING AND COPYRIGHT MANAGEMENT: BEST PRACTICES OF COLLEGE, SPECIAL, AND RESEARCH LIBRARIES
ISBN: 1-57440-068-1   Price: $80   Publication Date: May 2004

This report looks closely at the licensing and copyright-management strategies of a sample of leading research, college and special libraries and consortiums and includes interviews with leading experts. The focus is on electronic-database licensing, and includes discussions of the most pressing issues: development of consortiums and group buying initiatives, terms of access, liability for infringement, archiving, training and development, free-trial periods, contract language, contract-management software and time-management issues, acquiring and using usage statistics, elimination of duplication, enhancement of bargaining power, open-access publishing policies, interruption-of-service contingency arrangements, changes in pricing over the life of the contract, interlibrary loan of electronic files, copyright clearance, negotiating tactics, uses of consortiums, and many other issues. The report profiles the emergence of consortiums and group-buying arrangements.

CREATING THE DIGITAL ACADEMIC LIBRARY
ISBN: 1-57440-071-1   Price: $69.50   Publication Date: July 2004

This report looks closely at the efforts of more than 10 major academic libraries to develop their digital assets and deal with problems in the area of librarian time management, database selection, vendor relations, contract negotiation and tracking, electronic-resources funding and marketing, technical development, archival access, open access publishing agit prop, use of e-books, digitization of audio and image collections and other areas of the development of the digital academic library. The report includes profiles of Columbia University School of Medicine, the Health Sciences Complex of the University of Texas, Duke University Law Library, the University of Indiana Law Library, the University of South Carolina, the University of Idaho, and many others.

COLLEGE ALUMNI RELATIONS BENCHMARKS
Price: $295.00   Publication Date: 2007

This report gives critical data about the alumni relations efforts of North American colleges. In more than 115 pages and 400 tables, the study presents hard data on alumni affairs' office budgets, marketing expenditures, use of print publications and the Internet, directory building and fundraising activities, among other topics. The report, based on data from 60 colleges, gives the end-user highly specific benchmarking data such as the percentage of alumni that participate in reunions, earning from insurance plans and credit cards offered to alumni, spending on promotional materials for alumni clubs, percentage of alumni for whom the college maintains a working email address, and hundreds of other useful benchmarks and data points. Useful benchmarks include alumni office staff size, staff time spent on specific tasks, impact of the Internet on alumni communications, relations with the Office of Institutional Advancement, plans for the print directory and much more. Data are broken out for public and private colleges and by size and type of college and by size of the overall alumni population.

THE SURVEY OF DISTANCE LEARNING PROGRAMS IN HIGHER EDUCATION, 2007-08 EDITION
ISBN: 1-57440-087-8   Price: $129.50

The study is based on data from 45 higher education distance learning programs, with mean revenues of approximately $2.35 million. Data are broken out by size and type of college, for public and private colleges and for high, medium and low growth enrollment distance learning programs. The 200-page report presents more than 750 tables of data exploring many facets of distance learning programs, including revenues, cost structure, rates of pay, student demographics, program growth rates, current and planned use of new technologies, catering to special populations, and many other financial and business aspects of managing distance learning programs.

THE SURVEY OF COLLEGE MARKETING PROGRAMS
Price: $265.00   Publication Date: 2007

This report is based on detailed interviews with 55 America colleges. The report presents hard data on use of and spending on a broad range of promotional vehicles including direct mail, Web ads and Website sponsorships, email broadcasts, blog monitoring, search engine placement enhancement, newspaper and magazine ads, billboards, television and radio advertising, Website development and other forms of advertising.

The study also presents findings on use of and spending by colleges on marketing consultants such as market research agencies, public relations firms and advertising agencies, among others. In addition, the report explores the management and organization of the college's branding and promotional efforts, exploring the degree of centralization and other issues in the management of the college marketing effort.

TRENDS IN TRAINING COLLEGE FACULTY, STUDENTS & STAFF IN COMPUTER LITERACY
ISBN: 1-57440-085-1   Price: $67.50   Publication Date: April 2007

This report looks closely at how nine institutions of higher education are approaching the question of training faculty, staff and students in the use of educationally-oriented information technologies. The report helps answer questions such as: what is the most productive way to help faculty to master new information technologies? How much should be spent on such training? What are the best practices? How should distance learning instructors be trained? How formal, and how ad-hoc, should training efforts be? What should be computer literacy standards among students? How can subject specific computer literacy be integrated into curriculums? Should colleges develop their own training methods, buy packaged solutions, find them on the Web?

Organizations profiled include: Brooklyn Law School, Florida State University College of Medicine, Indiana University Southeast, Texas Christian University, Clemson University, the Teaching & Learning Technology Group, the Appalachian College Association, Tuskegee Institute and the University of West Georgia.

THE SURVEY OF LIBRARY CAFÉS
Price: $75.00   ISBN: 1-57440-089-4   Publication Date: 2007

The Survey of Library Cafés presents data from more than 40 academic and public libraries about their cafes and other foodservice operations. The 60-page report gives extensive data and commentary on library café sales volume, best-selling products, impacts on library maintenance costs, reasons for starting a café, effects on library traffic, and many other issues regarding the decision to start and manage a library café.

CORPORATE LIBRARY BENCHMARKS, 2007 Edition
ISBN: 1-57440-084-3   Price: $189.00

This report, our sixth survey of corporate libraries, presents a broad range of data, broken out by size and type of organization. Among the issues covered are: spending trends on books, magazines, journals, databases, CD-ROM, directories and other information vehicles, plans to augment or reduce the scope and size of the corporate library, hiring plans, salary spending and personnel use, librarian research priorities by type of subject matter, policies on information literacy and library education, library relations with management, budget trends, breakdown in spending by the library vs other corporate departments that procure information, librarian use of blogs and RSS feeds, level of discounts received from book jobbers, use of subscription agents and other issues of concern to corporate and other business librarians.

EMERGING ISSUES IN ACADEMIC LIBRARY CATALOGING & TECHNICAL SERVICES
ISBN: 1-57440-086-X   Price: $72.50   Publication Date: April 2007

This report presents nine highly detailed case studies of leading university cataloging and technical service departments. It provide insights into how they are handling 10 major changes facing them, including: the encouragement of cataloging productivity; impact of new technologies on and enhancement of online catalogs; the transition to metadata standards; the cataloging of Websites and digital and other special collections; library catalog and metadata training; database maintenance, holdings, and physical processing; managing the relationship with acquisitions departments; staff education; and other important issues. Survey participants represent academic libraries of varying sizes and classifications, with many different viewpoints. Universities surveyed are: Brigham Young; Curry College; Haverford College; Illinois, Louisiana and Pennsylvania State Universities; University of North Dakota; University of Washington; and Yale.

EMERGING BEST PRACTICES IN LEGAL RECORDS MANAGEMENT
Price: $295.00   Publication Date: March 2006
This special report is based on detailed interview with records managers, practice management directors and partners in major law firms and other legal offices. Among the organizational participants are: Kaye Scholer, Fulbright & Jawarski, Kilpatrick Stockton, Thomas Cooley Law School , the National Archives & Records Administration, Thompson Hine, Dewey Ballantine and Blackwell Sanders Peper Martin.

Among the issues covered in detail: Records Department Staff Size, Budget & Range of Responsibilities, Breakdown of Employee Time Use, Space Benchmarks for Offsite storage, Classification Scheme and Planning for Records Retrieval, Integration of Records with Copyright Information, Emails, Correspondence and other Forms of Legal Information, Types of Knowledge Management Software/Systems Under Consideration, Uses of Records Request Tracking, Strategies for Employee and Attorney Training in Content Control, USE of RFID & Barcoding Technology, Pace & Cost of Records Digitization, Digitization Technology & Storage Options, Records Security & Password Strategy, Relations Among the Library, Docket, Records Department, Information Technology Department and other Units Involved in Content/Knowledge Management and much more.

CORPORATE LIBRARY BENCHMARKS, 2005 EDITION
Price: 159.50   PDF Price: $174.50   Publication Date: October 2004
Corporate Library Benchmarks presents data from a survey of 50 major corporate and other business libraries. In more than 185 tables of data and commentary, the report charts developments in materials purchasing, use of office space, trends in use of librarian staff time, Fate of the physical library, trends in number of visitors to the library, trends in budgets, use of digital resources, role in knowledge management and many other facets of corporate librarianship. Data are broken out by major industry sector and by company size. Data contributed by many of America's leading corporations.

THE SURVEY OF LAW FIRM eMARKETING PRACTICES
Price: $295.00   Number of Tables: 120+
This study is based on a survey of 40 law firms with a mean size of 211 lawyers; data is broken out by size of law firm (by number of total lawyers) and by number of practice groups. Some data is also presented on a per partner basis, such as spending on Website development, per partner. In each firm a major marketing official answered questions

regarding editorial staff, Website development and marketing, use of blogs, listservs, eNewsletters and other cyberspace promotion and information vehicles.

The report presents hard data on the use of search engine placement consultants, click through rates on eNewsletters, number of unique visitors to the firm Website, and presents data on law firm spending plans for a broad range of eMarketing vehicles. The report presents hard data on law firm use of opt-in email, banner ads, Website sponsorship, per-click payments to Google, Yahoo, MSN and Overture, and much more.

The study also discusses the impact of Web-based press release distribution services and presents data on the number of law firms that use, and plan to use such services. In addition to examining the prevailing methods of eMarketing, the report looks at law firm intentions in emerging eMarketing methods such as podcasting, Webcasting and streaming video, among others. The report presents quantitative assessment data on the usefulness of specific online directory sites such as Law.com, Findlaw.com and Superpages.com.

LAW LIBRARY BENCHMARKS, 2006-07 Edition
Price: $119.50   Publication Date: April 2006
Data are broken out for law firm, university law school, and public sector law libraries. Some data is also broken out for corporate law departments. The report provides data from more than 80 major law libraries library and covers subjects such as staff size and growth, salaries and budget, spending trends in the library content budget, use of blogs, listservs and RSS feeds, spending on databases and commercial online services, use of and plans for CD-ROM, parent organization management's view of the future of the law library, assessment of attorney search skills, trends in information literacy training, use of reference tracking software and much more.